I0420997

Editor-in-Chief and Founder:
  Lyndon H. LaRouche, Jr.
Editorial Board: *Lyndon H. LaRouche, Jr. , Helga Zepp-LaRouche, Paul Gallagher, Tony Papert, Gerald Rose, Dennis Small, Jeffrey Steinberg, William Wertz*
Co-Editors: *Paul Gallagher, Tony Papert*
Managing Editor: *Nancy Spannaus*
Technology: *Marsha Freeman*
Books: *Katherine Notley*
Ebooks: *Richard Burden*
Graphics: *Alan Yue*
Photos: *Stuart Lewis*
Circulation Manager: *Stanley Ezrol*

INTELLIGENCE DIRECTORS
Counterintelligence: *Jeffrey Steinberg, Michele Steinberg*
Economics: *John Hoefle, Marcia Merry Baker, Paul Gallagher*
History: *Anton Chaitkin*
Ibero-America: *Dennis Small*
Russia and Eastern Europe: *Rachel Douglas*
United States: *Debra Freeman*

INTERNATIONAL BUREAUS
Bogotá: *Miriam Redondo*
Berlin: *Rainer Apel*
Copenhagen: *Tom Gillesberg*
Houston: *Harley Schlanger*
Lima: *Sara Madueño*
Melbourne: *Robert Barwick*
Mexico City: *Gerardo Castilleja Chávez*
New Delhi: *Ramtanu Maitra*
Paris: *Christine Bierre*
Stockholm: *Ulf Sandmark*
United Nations, N.Y.C.: *Leni Rubinstein*
Washington, D.C.: *William Jones*
Wiesbaden: *Göran Haglund*

ON THE WEB
e-mail: eirns@larouchepub.com
www.larouchepub.com
www.executiveintelligencereview.com
www.larouchepub.com/eiw
Webmaster: *John Sigerson*
Assistant Webmaster: *George Hollis*
Editor, Arabic-language edition: *Hussein Askary*

EIR (ISSN 0273-6314) *is published weekly (50 issues), by EIR News Service, Inc., P.O. Box 17390, Washington, D.C. 20041-0390. (703) 777-9451*

European Headquarters: E.I.R. GmbH, Postfach Bahnstrasse 9a, D-65205, Wiesbaden, Germany
Tel: 49-611-73650
Homepage: http://www.eirna.com
e-mail: eirna@eirna.com
Director: Georg Neudecker

Montreal, Canada: 514-461-1557

Denmark: EIR - Danmark, Sankt Knuds Vej 11, basement left, DK-1903 Frederiksberg, Denmark. Tel.: +45 35 43 60 40, Fax: +45 35 43 87 57. e-mail: eirdk@hotmail.com.

Mexico City: EIR, Sor Juana Inés de la Cruz 242-2 Col. Agricultura C.P. 11360 Delegación M. Hidalgo, México D.F. Tel. (5525) 5318-2301 eirmexico@gmail.com

We Have to Fight!

EIR Contents

www.larouchepub.com Volume 42, Number 33, August 21, 2015

Robert and Clara Schumann, 1847

White House Video

Cover This Week

Robert & Clara Schumann in 1847 by Eduard Kaiser.

We Have to Fight!

by Tony Papert

Aug. 13—We're being buffaloed by Obama, or what he represents. Although Obama's policy is a fast road to total destruction, including thermonuclear war probably this month,—yet people are adapting to it. They're tending to say, "It's hopeless; we have to submit."

This is what's killing us.

Americans have capitulated to two two-term Presidents: first Bush, and then Obama. Just think how many young people have come to maturity during those fifteen years? You're dealing with an entire generation which is intrinsically degenerate, because they never really knew anything. Our young people really have no understanding of anything. Young people and young adults just fall into it. A whole oldest generation has died out in the meantime, and this one replaced it. As the result, the population has lost all comprehension of what has been happening, as the whole society has tilted sharply into this capitulation. The whole society is based on an adaptation to it.

We have a nation with a lot of people who do have guts, but the population reads the signs, and they follow the signs. A whole population goes down that road, and they're buffaloed. We simply have to work against popular opinion,—against the stupidity which dominates popular opinion. What dominates the population is their cultivated stupidity. Especially, we must work against the acceptance of it by people who should know better.

An entire system of belief has grown up among us, which is secretly (or not-so secretly) based on caving in to the adaptation to Bush, and then Obama. Among those Americans who more than any others should know better, nearly all of them have succumbed to it internally. It's obvious. To try to assuage their consciences, they trap themselves in precious private opinions. Petty private projects. They preoccupy themselves with precious, little private gripes. All these are fetishes, with which they wall themselves off from the real issues of life, which they ignore. They make themselves completely incompetent,— deliberately. We cave in to the things which oppress us, a tendency which is especially strong south of the Mason-Dixon line, where evil is most concentrated.

You can't blame the population for this: blame yourself! Whether for embodying this blindness, or for accommodating to it. Those for whom there is any hope, will begin by privately recognizing the truth of this description.

Now, Hillary Clinton's political and moral degeneration has been a bellwether for the moral degeneration of the population.

Anyone who refuses to immediately re-introduce Franklin Roosevelt's Glass-Steagall protections, must be excluded as a candidate. It represents the moral difference between foolish ideas and the interests of humanity.

Hillary Clinton began to degenerate morally when Bill Clinton was whipsawed by the Queen of England, operating through the Republican Party, in his second term. Hillary adapted to what was done to him; she didn't recognize that it was an operation, didn't recognize that it was the Queen of England behind it. She adapted to what was done to Bill. Then she disregarded LaRouche's advice to stay in the U.S. Senate rather than become Obama's Secretary of State. Obama bullied her into concession after concession, retreat after retreat. On Sept 11, 2012, he bullied her into covering for his criminality on Benghazi; Obama's impeachment should have begun on very that day.

Now, Hillary is a failure. There's no future for her. And Obama has teamed up with the Bush family against her. They won't be content with denying her the nomination: both Obama and the Bushes want her in prison, for a start,—and then probably want her dead. The only thing she can do to have a future, is to finally tell the truth about Obama and Benghazi. Obama's impeachment should have begun on that day of Sept 11, 2012,—but it was hushed up. Let it begin now, Hillary! Let it begin today, before Obama can launch the thermonuclear war towards which he's aiming.

Lyndon LaRouche launched the Manhattan Project in October, 2014, to pick an area of organizing the nation; a leadership impulse from a relevant part of the nation. Take that, and you have a point of mobilization for the larger population. The problem is not just the South as such, but that people adapt to the South. That Manhattan Project is succeeding, and it will succeed if you give it the time. We have to fight.

The Example of Robert and Clara Schumann

by Harley Schlanger

People who are practical are intrinsically tragic, because they limit themselves to what they think is practical, whereas progress is always based on getting beyond being practical, by making discoveries of principle, or discovering principles which had existed before, but you didn't understand them.

—Lyndon LaRouche, August 16, 2015

Aug 18—While Lyndon LaRouche was commenting on the cowardice and moral degeneration which characterizes today's political leaders, as well as the general population, his observation applies to the human condition, throughout history. Improvements in the conditions of mankind have always been the result of the creative intervention of small numbers of courageous individuals, who rejected submission to arbitrary power, who defied popular opinion, and who refused to adapt to the fears and smallness of those around them. For such improvements, it has been necessary to wage war, not just against the oligarchical forces which have oppressed the vast majority, but also against the tendency of ordinary citizens to submit and retreat, in the face of what appear to be overwhelming obstacles.

How can small people, used to submission, be

"He who does not attack the bad, defends the good but halfway," wrote Robert Schumann. Here he is depicted in a lithograph by Josef Kriehuber in 1839.

moved to act for a higher purpose?

LaRouche has been emphasizing that people must be mobilized to *think*, rather than merely reacting, out of anger and frustration. The most effective means to accomplish this is through the use of Classical culture as a weapon, in particular Classical music, which, when properly performed, enables members of an audience to get a glimpse into the beautiful mind of a creative artist, and to participate, in a way, in the act of creation. And when one is able to participate more directly, by performing in a chorus, singing great works by the most accomplished composers, in that Classical method, the effect is further enhanced—the performer becomes directly involved in an act of creation, and is able to experience what it means to be creative.

Such an experience, of direct, personal involvement in the discovery of principles, is the strongest weapon against the induced littleness of those who live, as we do today, in a degenerating culture. Once one has gone through that experience, the willingness and ability to combat degeneracy is greatly increased. That is the weapon being unleashed in the development of a chorus, in New York City, as a central feature of LaRouche's Manhattan Project.

Robert Schumann's War

One individual who understood this creative power, and dedicated his life to its propagation, in spite of great personal difficulties associated with a debilitating illness, as well as opposition from networks run by the oligarchy, was Robert Schumann (1810-1856). Schumann organized around him a small group of musicians and other artists, intent on using their art to attack the destructive, superficial culture of their time, while demonstrating the higher capacity for creative discovery, which alone can open the door to a better future for all mankind. In April 1834, at the age of 24, Schumann launched a publication, "Neue Zeitschrift für Musik" ("New Journal of Music"), to defend and promote the Classical musical tradition of J.S. Bach, Mozart, and Beethoven, which was under assault by the proponents of "new music," with its emphasis on virtuoso technique and emotional effect.

In its first issue, Schumann declared war on these networks, which he characterized as modern Philistines.

> He who does not attack the bad, defends the good but halfway. Our purpose... is to remind our readers emphatically of the distant past and its works. Then, to emphasize the fact that the contemporary artist can secure strength for the creation of new beauty only by drinking from such pure fountains. Then, to attack as inartistic the immediate past, which is concerned merely with encouraging superficial virtuosity. Lastly, to help prepare and hasten the coming of a new poetic era.

His publication served as a rallying point for those who feared that, with the deaths of Beethoven (1827) and Schubert (1828), the Classical tradition would be buried. As Schumann knew well, the great composers of the past had been targeted by bought-and-paid-for critics, who claimed that their music was inaccessible to the common man, and who conspired to prevent the performance of their works.

In collaboration with his wife Clara, and with Felix Mendelssohn, Johannes Brahms, and others, Schumann and his allies not only defended the heritage of Bach against such inane slander, but produced new beautiful works. They organized concerts and choruses, and recruited the best performers, such as the violinist Joseph Joachim, to their circle, to bring these musical ideas to a new generation. They studied the compositional methods of the Bach tradition, such as fugal counterpoint, and applied and developed them. In doing so,

"My entire political creed consists of nothing but the bloodiest hatred for our whole civilization...," wrote Richard Wagner. This photo was taken by Franz Hanfstaengl in 1870.

they demonstrated that music does not reside in a succession of notes, as a sensuous effect, but is produced in the mind, as a means of accessing the higher mental faculties of what LaRouche calls "creativity per se."

For this small network, this was a moral fight, a war to lift man above mere sensuality—a state in which a population is easy to manipulate and control—to a dialogue with the Deity. Schumann wrote, "For me, music is always the language which permits one to converse with the Beyond." In a direct attack on his contemporaries, Franz Liszt and Richard Wagner, for whom producing an effect in the lower extremities was their specialty, he wrote polemically that the "most important thing is for the musician to purify his inner ear."

Battling the Satanic

Schumann's death in 1856 left to his wife and Brahms, primarily, the responsibility to take on the evil represented by Liszt and Wagner. These latter two were promoted by the degenerate oligarchs of Europe, who created a virtual cult around them, in order to wipe out the Classical tradition.

In his anti-Semitic screed attacking Mendelssohn and Meyerbeer, "Judaism in Music," published in September 1850, Wagner explicitly identified his target as the Classical compositional method, championed by Schumann:

> Do what you will: look away from Beethoven, fumble after Mozart, gird yourself round with Johann Sebastian Bach: write symphonies with or without choruses, write masses, oratorios—sexless opera-embryos!—make songs without words, operas without texts!.... We look without fear toward that great annihilating blow of destiny which will make an end of this whole unwieldy

monstrosity of music, clearing space for the Artwork of the Future.

Wagner's nihilistic view was not limited to the great Classical composers, but to all mankind, as he admitted in a letter written in 1851:

My entire political creed consists of nothing but the bloodiest hatred for our whole civilization, contempt for all things deriving from it, and a longing for nature.... In Europe, I prefer dogs to these dog-like men.... Only the most horrific and destructive revolution could make our civilized beasts 'human' again.

It is not coincidental that Wagner was revered by Hitler and leading Nazis, nor that he expresses the same contempt for mankind that one finds in the likes of the pro-genocidal Prince Philip, of the Nazi-loving British Royal Family!

Clara Schumann and Brahms engaged in direct combat with Liszt and Wagner, openly identifying them as a destructive force. Of Liszt, Clara wrote in her diary:

He played, as always, with a truly demonic bravura and possessed the piano really like a devil (I cannot express it any other way)... but oh, his compositions, that was really too horrible.

Of Wagner, she wrote of his "Rheingold," "I felt as if I were wading in a swamp the whole evening.... The boredom one must endure, however, is dreadful." She described attending a performance of "Tristan und Isolde," with its love/death theme, as "the saddest thing I have experienced in my entire artistic life."

New Musical Principles

This battle against the Satanic efforts of Liszt and Wagner, and their sponsors, was by no means limited to criticizing their works, but meant the discovery of new musical principles in the tradition of Bach. One profound example of this is Brahms' *"Ein Deutsches Requiem"* ("A German Requiem"), which premiered in Leipzig in February 1869, as Chancellor Otto von Bismarck's unification of Germany was moving toward its successful

"Study Bach. There you will find everything," wrote Schumann collaborator Johannes Brahms. This photo was taken in 1853.

conclusion. Using a text from the Lutheran Bible in German, rather than a Latin text, and incorporating Bachian counterpoint throughout, Brahms' work was quite popular, as it inspired a pride in Germans, as well as a humility, in challenging the living to act to continue the mission of those who have departed.

This elevating and actually human treatment of immortality pointed listeners to the future, something which was intolerable for Wagner, whose "dramas" were designed to glorify a non-existent past, in a world in which destruction was the highest good. Wagner said derisively about Brahms' Requiem, "We will want no German Requiem to be played to our ashes."

While it may appear that the sponsors of Liszt and Wagner succeeded, as Brahms was the last composer in this tradition, and the musical culture of the Twentieth Century has been one of accelerating degeneration, theirs is a pyrrhic victory. The battle to enhance the creative power of man, through defending and promoting Classical culture, which was the focal point of existence for the Schumann circle, was kept alive, through the efforts of the towering figure of Classical music in the 20th Century, Wilhelm Furtwängler, and his allies.

Today, through the work of Lyndon LaRouche, and his organizing of the Manhattan Project, we can draw inspiration from the insistence of the Schumann circle on fighting on, against the destructive evil represented by Liszt and Wagner. The choral principle, which is at the heart of LaRouche's Manhattan Project, is a revival of the heroic work of that small circle of geniuses which emerged around Robert Schumann. The future of humanity depends on the ability of such small circles today to organize, with the commitment to the ennoblement of mankind, which was the mission embraced by Robert and Clara Schumann.

For Further Reading:
"Robert and Clara Schumann, and Their Teacher, J.S. Bach," by Michelle Rasmussen, *EIR*, June 18, 2010.
"The Musical Soul of Scientific Creativity: Rebecca Dirichlet's Development of the Complex Domain," by David Shavin, *EIR*, June 10, 2010.

Is the FBI Running You? Are You Sure?

by Barbara Boyd

Aug 16—On August 25, 1967, J. Edgar Hoover, the racist, closeted-homosexual, southern masonic monster who ran the FBI, America's very own Gestapo organization, dictated the following memo, titled "Counterintelligence Program, Black Nationalist Hate Groups, Internal Security."

The purpose of this new counterintelligence endeavor is to expose, disrupt, misdirect, discredit, or **otherwise neutralize** the activities of black nationalist hate-type organizations and groupings, their leadership, spokesmen, membership, and supporters, and to counter their propensity for violence and civil disorder.... The pernicious background of such groups, their duplicity, and devious maneuvers must be exposed to public scrutiny where such publicity will have a **neutralizing** effect. Efforts of the various groups to consolidate their forces or to recruit new or youthful adherents must be frustrated. **No opportunity should be missed to exploit through counterintelligence techniques the organizational and personal conflicts of the leaderships of the groups** and where possible an effort should be made to capitalize upon existing conflicts between competing black nationalist organizations....

When an opportunity is apparent to disrupt or neutralize ... through the cooperation of established local news media contacts or through such contact with sources at the Seat of Government" (Hoover's office) ... "careful attention must be paid to ensure the targeted group is disrupted, ridiculed, or discredited through the publicity, and not merely publicized. (emphasis added)

By March 4, 1968, Hoover further clarified the goals of the program as follows:

1. *Prevent the coalition of militant black nationalist groups. "An effective coalition might be the first step toward a real 'Mau Mau' black revolutionary army in America."*

2. *Prevent the rise of a "Messiah" who could unify and electrify the black nationalist movement. "Malcolm X might have been such a messiah.... Martin Luther King, Stokely Carmichael, and Elijah Muhammed all aspire to this position."*

3. *Prevent militant black nationalists from gaining respectability by discrediting them to three separate sections of the community—"the responsible Negro community," the "white commu-*

Marion S Trikosko

J. Edgar Hoover, director of the Federal Bureau of Investigation (FBI) from its founding in 1935, to his death in 1972.

creative commons/ Matthew W. Hutchins

George Bush Presidential Library and Museum

In Hoover's footsteps: George H.W. Bush, who served as CIA Director, Vice President, President; and Cass Sunstein, President Obama's legal advisor and former Administrator of his Office of Information and Regulatory Affairs.

nity including the 'responsible community' and 'liberals' who sympathize with black nationalists because they are Negroes," and third, "these groups must be discredited in the eyes of Negro radicals, the followers of the movement."

"A final goal should be to prevent the long-range growth of militant black organizations, especially among youth."

The terminology provided by Hoover shouldn't mislead anyone. He included as violent Black Nationalists, Martin Luther King's specifically non-violent Southern Christian Leadership Conference, for example.

By May 5, 1968, Hoover had formally opened the same program against the anti-Vietnam war movement, entitled, "COINTELPRO New Left," disruption of the New Left. Lyndon LaRouche's National Caucus of Labor Committees was targeted in "COINTELPRO New Left," and by 1973-74 had become one of two primary political organizational targets of FBI counterintelligence targeting, although the formal COINTELPRO program had ended by that time.[1]

Into the Daylight

On March 7, 1971, anti-war activists broke in to FBI offices in Media, Pennsylvania, stealing files which bore the then-mysterious heading "COINTELPRO," and

then leaked them to the press. It was the beginning of the end of J. Edgar Hoover's career-long effort, in parallel with Army intelligence, a host of Wall Street and government-funded private organizations, and, in later years, the Dulles brothers' CIA, to pacify the population of the United States. Richard Nixon's "Watergate" scandal, leaked to the *Washington Post* by Mark Felt, a high-ranking Hoover protégé turned apostate, followed.

Amongst other revelations, Americans learned that for years the news media had been feeding them an artificial picture of key people and events, based on journalists and media companies, such as CBS, NBC, the *Washington Post*, and the *New York Times*, producing stories dictated by the FBI, CIA, and Wall Street-sponsored public relations experts. The image of the square-jawed, honest FBI man, projected by Hoover's PR machine in comic books, popular magazines and fiction, major motion pictures and television productions, and sold to the American public, turned out to be an awful satanic fraud.

But, the program did not end, obviously, with Hoover. Yes, there was a great hue and cry at the time, and heads rolled. President Nixon was forced to resign. But, the programs and, more importantly, the policies involved, were only partially exposed and reformed.

George H.W. Bush, first as President Ford's CIA Director, and then as Vice-President under Reagan, led the effort to obscure and conceal essential matters from Congress, and to reverse the intelligence reforms initiated in the wake of the Watergate scandal. The top-secret domestic counterintelligence programs were re-

---

1. The documents are available on the FBI website. Go to the Vault or FBI Reading Room, find COINTELPRO in the index, and click on the subfile Black Nationalist Extremist Groups.

established at that time under E.O. 12333 and related orders, and remain classified. The post September 11, 2001 security world finds various Republican intelligence training think tanks comfortably asserting that J. Edgar Hoover "had it about right" when it comes to the internal security of the United States. They excuse his notorious and visceral racism as "context,"—the natural effect of growing up in the very southern Washington, D.C. at the time he did.

Not to be outdone, Obama's constitutional law guru Cass Sunstein, husband to Obama's fanatical UN Ambassador Samantha Power, casually advocates, in a 2009 *Journal of Political Philosophy* piece,[2] that the government infiltrate any group advocating "conspiracy theories," especially those who don't believe the Bush/Cheney Administration's cover story about 9/11, in

Rev. Martin Luther King, one of Hoover's key targets, addresses the August 2, 1963 March on Washington.

order to create "cognitive dissonance." He also speaks of "neutralization" in this context, as does Obama's FBI, repeatedly, with respect to alleged terrorists. Sunstein has otherwise argued that federal judges should not interpret federal laws—that task is uniquely that of the President and those around him. This is the unconstitutional theory of the unitary executive, a guiding assumption of everything Hoover and his associates said or did.

"Neutralization"

The Church and Pike Committee Congressional Hearings of 1975-76 revealed that during the FBI's COINTELPRO programs, and the parallel programs run by Army Intelligence, the CIA ("Operation Chaos"), and the NSA (Operation Minaret), dissident political leaders in the United States were subjected to numerous false arrests and imprisonment, defamation to family, friends, and potential associates, burglaries and thefts, unauthorized wiretaps, bugs, and NSA surveillance, assassinations, and gang-versus-countergang orchestrated murders. FBI informants flooded targeted organizations—alerted to transcribe personal flaws, gossip, organizational intrigue, family, sexual, and financial practices and problems—all for exploitation by the FBI

2. Sunstein, Cass R, Vermeule, Adrian (June 2009), "Conspiracy Theories, Causes and Cures." *Journal of Political Philosophy* (Wiley)17(2): 202-227.

or other intelligence operatives.

Mail was opened, documents were stolen in black bag jobs, employers and family were visited and warned. Blackmail acquired by criminal and sexual entrapments, fear of publicity concerning sexual and financial misdeeds, and fear of FBI-created familial estrangements, were used to break cadre in these organizations, turning them into FBI informants. FBI informants were put into positions of leadership in some of the targeted organizations, further enhancing the capacity to disrupt and "neutralize."

To recall but a few examples. The FBI famously claimed to record, via a surreptitiously placed bug, Martin Luther King's extramarital sexual encounters. Hoover and friends played the tapes for President Johnson and various Bureau-controlled Washington, D.C. reporters, in a quest to plant the ultimate newspaper story which would destroy King. No one jumped on the story.

Hoover then ordered that the tapes be mailed to King and his wife, together with an anonymous letter suggesting King commit suicide lest the tapes be publicly revealed. This idea apparently occurred to Hoover when *Time Magazine* revealed, in a lead article on King, that King had twice attempted suicide while an adolescent. According to author Curt Gentry, Hoover already had a replacement in mind to lead the "black movement,"—New York lawyer Samuel Pierce.

The Black Panther Party for Self-Defense was riddled with informants from its inception. When it was recently documented that the first person to suggest that the Panthers use guns, providing them to the Panther leadership, was an FBI informant, former leaders of the group denied this possibility, and instead insisted that the individual had been snitch-jacketed, a favored FBI technique. Using its assets, the FBI often suggested individuals were informants, when they were not, simply to discredit the individuals, or place them in physical danger. As a result of Hoover's COINTELPRO directive, the Panthers, Ron Karenga's United Slaves (U.S.) organization, and the criminal gang, the Black P. Stone Rangers, were set up in FBI-orchestrated gang warfare in which many people were killed, "neutralized."

Paradigm of Control

The 1960s FBI counterinsurgency tactics were taken from the Hoover and Army G2 post-World War II war on "communism" and "socialism," following the death of the great Franklin Roosevelt and the ascent of the vicious and mob-tinged little man from Missouri, Harry S Truman. The COINTELPRO operation against the Communist Party was the first formal program so titled by Hoover for these illegal activities. In his book on Hoover, Curt Gentry documents that Hoover and the Army's G2 effectively ran the House Un-American Activities Committee (HUAC), and Joe McCarthy and his shyster lawyer Roy Cohn, feeding them all their targets and dirt, although this collaboration was completely denied at the time.[3]

In his pursuit of "subversives," Hoover enjoyed a long-standing relationship with American organized crime, which actually shared his worldview and fed him information. In addition, among his closest confidants and informants were a network of American Catholics, centered in the New York archdiocese and its Cardinal Spellman, itself deeply entangled with organized crime.

Public objections to Hoover's witchhunts, like those voiced by New Jersey Congressman Neil Gallagher, were met with legal frameups and social ostracism. While it is true that Hoover protected his personal position by using his huge network of agents and informants to gather blackmail information on every President he served under, together with most members of Congress, his famous files were not solely responsible for his long

tenure in his position. He was completely personally funded by Wall Street's Texas networks, Clint Murchison and Sid Richardson, the same networks which gave birth to George H.W. Bush and family. This was not accidental. The historical sketch we provide below demonstrates that he was a created and protected tool of the Anglo-American oligarchy.

Since Hoover's death in 1972, the objectives of this oligarchy have not changed, although their tactics have shifted. Beginning with the assassination of John F. Kennedy in 1963, the Anglo-Americans have relied increasingly on more directed forms of psychological warfare, basing their strategies on the group- and mass-psychological control studies produced by Kurt Lewin, Eric Trist, and their mass-brainwashing successors. The successive psychological shocks of assassinations of political leaders, terrorist assaults, the rock-drug-sex counterculture, and the internet "revolution," have produced an increasingly atomized, infantile, degenerate, and autistic culture, in which cultural barriers have become the key factor preventing significant social change.

This is what was intended by the National Training Institute and Tavistock Institute studies of group dynamics and mass behavior. In this new paradigm, there is no need for droves of paid informants, because potential targets reveal all of their deepest secrets on public social media sites. There is no need for burglaries to place bugs, when the NSA routinely scoops up everything their targets say or do.

The 20th Century British Drive
To Recolonize the United States

What does COINTELPRO itself mean? Formally, it is "counterintelligence program." This program, we will show, comes from the "counterinsurgency" matrix of British imperialism, the policing of subject populations to ensure against any form of popular revolt, or, once an insurgency has taken root, to crush it—by mostly non-conventional military means, always with the option, however, of using lethal force.

COINTELPRO is a war against the population, aimed at controlling public opinion, and isolating and eliminating those who dissent from the allowed public myths and constructs. This is what is meant by "winning hearts and minds." If you take Hoover's "COINTELPRO Black Nationalist Hate Groups'" targeting of Martin Luther King, the SCLC, and others, cited above, and compare it to any modern military manual concern-

---

3. Gentry, Curt, *J. Edgar Hoover: The Man and His Secrets*, W.W. Norton Company, Inc., New York, 1991.

ing counterinsurgency, the tactics and intent are the same.

Curt Gentry's recent book on Hoover, and the work of Alfred McCoy,[4] have located the authorship of the Hoover/FBI, Army-G2 post-World War II American counterinsurgency with one Ralph Van Deman, widely credited with creating U.S. Army Intelligence. Van Deman was Hoover's counterintelligence mentor. While the history of this effort is beyond the scope of the present article, my colleague Tony Chaitkin is working on an article which will cover this Twentieth Century subversion of the United States in significant detail.

Lyndon LaRouche has emphasized, however, that the real roots of the FBI's COINTELPRO, lie in the 1901 assassination of President William McKinley, and Bertrand Russell's and David Hilbert's world-wide attack on the scientific outlook, beginning in 1900. The American system of government depends upon a strong and good presidential system, led by an inspired leader who challenges the nation to create a better future. The scientific world-view, exemplified by Gottfried Leibniz and embraced by Hamilton, Washington, and Franklin at the founding of the Republic, was responsible for the nation's great economic progress,—it was the driver of what Hamilton envisioned as the American System of economics.

Following McKinley's assassination, Americans were subjected to a string of London-controlled traitors as presidents—Teddy Roosevelt, Woodrow Wilson, and Calvin Coolidge. The depravity of these presidencies is illustrated by Woodrow Wilson's reviving the Ku Klux Klan directly from the White House. In the wake of the McKinley assassination, the British moved quickly through their Morgan and Rockefeller U.S. interests, in the coup against American System principles which resulted in the income tax, the Federal Reserve, and Wall Street's consolidation of control of American industry.

As part of this coup, Edward Bernays and Walter Lippmann created modern "public relations," or impe-

Hoover mentor Ralph Van Deman (1865-1952), known as the "Father of American Military Intelligence."

rial propaganda aimed at social control through "public opinion." Both voiced the view that the general public is incapable of exercising reasoned judgment, and consent must be engineered by an elite class of experts, using propaganda. These experts must be employed as a professional intelligence corps to guide the government. Lippmann directly acknowledged his debt to H.G. Wells' *Mankind in the Making* for his book-length screed on this issue, *Public Opinion.*

Working directly with the same Morgan and Rockefeller interests, under British agent and Texan Edward House in the Wilson Administration, Claude Dansey, a satanic and thoroughly evil British intelligence agent, was deployed to Washington, D.C. as the United States entered World War I. Dansey had previously recruited many on Wall Street *directly* to his MI6 networks.

In Washington, Ralph Van Deman, Marlborough Churchill, and Dansey modeled the U.S. Army's G-2 explicitly on British intelligence and counterinsurgency methods. Van Deman had employed these methods while in the U.S. military in the Philippines. He subsequently deployed himself to British colonial India to gain further first-hand experience. Van Deman remained one of Hoover's closest confidants until his death in 1952. In coordination with Hoover and G-2, he ran countless private citizen and group vigilante opera-

---

4. McCoy, Arthur, *Policing America's Empire,* University of Wisconsin Press, Madison, Wisconsin, 2009.

tions (including the American Protective League, the American Legion, and the Daughters of the American Revolution) against alleged Communists, other left-wing "subversives," trade unionists, and ethnic groups, all of which, as organized forces, Van Deman viewed as potential threats.

How Does This Work?

Unless a maverick political organization possesses a highly intelligent, fearless, and creative leader, coupled with a true scientific and self-critical culture and a shared truly revolutionary mission, it will, eventually, crumble under the pressures imposed by counterinsurgency operations. These operations are all designed to amplify the social pressures against new or unorthodox political and social views emanating from society generally. Lyndon LaRouche noted this in the early formation of his Labor Committees, citing "centrism" as the essential group dynamic to be defeated:

"The grave problem facing the revolutionary individual is his customary isolation from the overwhelming majority of society. He becomes a pariah. He is under grave social pressure to find a new organization to sustain his sense of social identity in place of the withdrawn or threatened sustenance he would normally seek in other parochialist institutions."

Under conditions of attack, the defense of the existence of the group itself, rather than continually creating and acting upon the principled agreements upon which the group is based, becomes the individual's primary and all-consuming focus. Within the group, various factions emerge which, in turn, mediate the individual's relationship to the group, as a whole. "Belonging" to the subgroup for shared reasons of organizational grievance, replaces the individual's principled reasons for joining the organization in the first place. Thus, under conditions of government attack, the organization's goals in practice become increasingly issue-based and parochial, smaller and smaller. Interest groups pursue their own self-interested policies with the passion formerly reserved for the revolutionary goals and program of the group as a whole.[5]

Almost all of the American organizations subjected to the counterinsurgency of the 1960s and early '70s lacked the prerequisites to survive and defeat the gov-

Library of Congress

Albert Einstein (1879-1955) said on numerous occasions: "My life is divided between equations and politics."

ernment's onslaught. Most important, they lacked a compelling vision for creating a future society, and a sound epistemological basis for their programs. Instead, their programs mostly consisted of an array of parochial demands.

When the Ford Foundation and others introduced and funded "local control" community organizing as the means to subvert the potential political awakening of the 1960s, offering so-called radicals a means to maintain their image without the trouble of an actually revolutionary viewpoint, most "New Left" organizers collapsed into aspirational Alinskyite groups, engineering minor reforms which did nothing to really change the lives of the people they claimed to serve. In fact, many of the former radicals became the new, friendlier, colonial administrators in such unchanging landscapes as America's ghettoes.

A Most Refreshing Counterpoint: The Case of Albert Einstein

Albert Einstein was stalked by Hoover beginning in the early 1930s and pursued relentlessly until Ein-

---

5. LaRouche, Lyndon, "Centrism as a Social Phenomenon, How Not To Build a Revolutionary Party," *Campaigner*, Vol. 3, No. 1, New York, 1970.

stein's death. In fact, Hoover considered his inability to pin the "red" and "spy" labels on Einstein or demoralize him in any respect, one of his great failures. Nonetheless, Einstein was barred from the Manhattan Project by the FBI and G2, had his household thoroughly infiltrated and bugged, his mail opened, his friendships and employers abused and scrutinized, and his immigration status challenged in a secret effort to deport him.

What stands out in author Fred Jerome's account of Hoover's actions, is Einstein's attitude toward the witchhunt—mocking, defiant, constantly using his own stature in creative defense of his political ideas and his friends. It is as if, like Ho Chi Minh and Gandhi, he had scientifically mapped the central features of Anglo-American counterinsurgency strategy, and set out with a deliberate and bold plan to find and exploit its weaknesses and defeat it.[6]

The mostly-empty canonization of the great scientist which is taught in our schools, leaves out Einstein's political being. He said, on numerous occasions, "My life is divided between equations and politics." According to Jerome, he published at least 195 political essays and articles on political topics, with 150 of his interviews, letters, and speeches quoted in the *New York Times* alone.

A ruthless anti-fascist, Einstein saw fascism, not Communism or the Soviet Union, as the gravest threat to the world. In the United States he ardently opposed racism in all of its ugly guises. He was a supporter of the Lincoln Brigade's battle against the fascist Franco in Spain, a sponsor of numerous Jewish scientists seeking refuge from Hitler, a supporter of Israel provided it reached a just accommodation with its Arab population, and a close friend of Eleanor Roosevelt and Paul Robeson, both of them major targets of Hoover.

Einstein was initially targeted by the Women's Patriot Corporation, one of the more bizarre private police organizations created in the wake of World War I. It opposed giving women the right to vote, among other right-wing causes, and was run by the wives of prominent East Coast bankers and families. By 1932, the mission of this group had become guarding America's borders against undesirables—communists, pacifists, feminists—and Einstein was at the top of their list. A largely phony, completely hysterical, and almost completely fabricated dossier on Einstein was compiled by a Mrs. Randolph Frothingham (I promise you, I am not making this up), and forwarded to the State Department and the press.

When Einstein heard about the dossier in the press, he mocked it on the front page of the *New York Times* of December 4, 1932:

"Never yet have I experienced from the fair sex such rejection of all advances; or, if I have, never from so many at once. But are they not perfectly right, these watchful citizenesses? Why should one open one's doors to a person who devours hard-boiled capitalists with as much appetite as the ogre Minotaur in Crete once devoured luscious Greek maidens—a person who is also so vulgar as to oppose every sort of war, except the inevitable one with one's own wife? Therefore, give heed to your clever and patriotic women folk and remember that the capital of mighty Rome was once saved by the cackling of its fateful geese."

Yet, as Jerome tells the story, the dossier resulted in the interrogation of Einstein and his wife, Elsa, by State Department officials on the eve of Einstein leaving Germany for what was planned to be a half-year appointment to Princeton in 1932. When the Berlin consular official asked Einstein whether he was a Communist or an anarchist, according to the Associated Press account at the time, "Professor Einstein's patience broke. His usual genial face stern and his normally melodious voice strident, he cried: 'What's this, an inquisition? Is this an attempt at chicanery? I don't propose to answer such questions. I didn't ask to go to America. Your countrymen invited me, yes, begged me. If I am to enter your country as a suspect, I don't want to go at all. If you don't want to give me a visa, please say so, and then I'll know where I stand.'"

Einstein walked out of the meeting, and called the consulate back, demanding his visa in 24 hours lest he cancel his trip. Elsa, his wife, called the press, including the *New York Times* and Associated Press, providing a blow by blow account. Elsa noted that Einstein said, "Wouldn't it be funny if they didn't let me in? The whole world would be laughing at America."

---

6. Jerome, Fred, *The Einstein File: J. Edgar Hoover's Secret War Against the World's Most Famous Scientist*, St. Martin's Press, New York, 2002. All of the quoted materials in this section are drawn directly from Fred Jerome's excellent account.

In Washington, following the calls from reporters, the State Department announced that Einstein's visa would be issued the next day. In New York City, the wife of the president of General Motors convened a meeting of prominent women who demanded, "on behalf of the intelligent American people," the recall of the consular official who interrogated Einstein and the rebuke of any in the State Department who gave credence to the "absurd" Frothingham dossier.

Fearless

Nonetheless, the phony Frothingham dossier was incorporated by Hoover into Einstein's FBI file, becoming a part of Einstein's official existence for years. As Jerome documents, many of the other allegations Hoover floated through Einstein's FBI file came straight from Nazi intelligence sources. This was not accidental, as Wall Street and London initially sponsored Hitler's rise to power in Germany, and swooned over Mussolini's fascism. Heinrich Himmler was on J. Edgar Hoover's "special correspondents'" list until 1939, an open fraternization only surpassed by that of John Foster Dulles.

Einstein's activities on behalf of the Lincoln Brigades drew the ire of Cardinal Spellman and the New York Catholic archdiocese who supported Franco. Spellman was, of course, one of Hoover's key New York City assets.

Perhaps nothing better demonstrates Einstein's fearless confrontation with Hoover's police-state than his public confrontation with the McCarthy witchhunt in 1953. On June 12th, he published a letter in the *New York Times* urging intellectuals not to testify before the red-hunting Congressional committees.

Reactionary politicians have managed to instill suspicion of all intellectual efforts into the public by dangling before their eyes a danger from without. Having succeeded so far, they are now proceeding to suppress the freedom of teaching

'Refuse to Testify,' Einstein Advises Intellectuals Called In by Congress

By LEONARD BUDER

Dr. Albert Einstein, in a letter made public yesterday, said that every intellectual called before a Congressional investigating committee should refuse to testify, and "must be prepared for jail and economic ruin, in short, for the sacrifice of his personal welfare in the interest of the cultural welfare of his country."

He declared that "it is shameful for a blameless citizen to submit to such an inquisition," and that "this kind of inquisition violates the spirit of the Constitution."

The world's foremost physicist made his views known in an exchange of correspondence with a New York teacher of English who is facing dismissal from the school system because of his refusal to testify before the Senate Internal Security subcommittee. The teacher, William Frauenglass of James Madison High School, made public Dr. Einstein's letter, which bore

the postscript that it need not be considered confidential.

Reached by telephone at his home in Princeton, N. J., Dr. Einstein confirmed the letter, which was read to him. He said, in response to a question, that he would refuse to testify if called before a Congressional committee.

Mr. Frauenglass, a high school teacher for more than twenty-three years, wrote to Dr. Einstein on May 9 and referred to a statement the scientist had made recently in which he described himself as "an incorrigible nonconformist" in a "remote field of endeavor" that no Senatorial committee had as yet felt impelled to tackle.

The Brooklyn teacher then related that on April 24 he had been called before the Senate subcommittee as a result of lectures he had given six years earlier at an

Continued on Page 9, Column 2

From the New York Times, June 12, 1953.

and to deprive of their positions all those who do not prove submissive, i.e., to starve them out.

What ought the minority of intellectuals do against this evil? Frankly, I can only see the revolutionary way of non-cooperation in the sense of Gandhi's. Every intellectual who is called before the committees ought to refuse to testify, i.e., must be prepared for jail and economic ruin, in short for the sacrifice of his personal welfare in the interest of the cultural welfare of this country.

If enough people are ready to take this grave step, they will be successful. If not, then the intellectuals deserve nothing better than the slavery which is intended for them.

Einstein was immediately attacked in virulent editorials by the *New York Times* and *Washington Post*. Ultimately, however, his letter helped sparked the resistance which led to the downfall of Hoover's pawns, Joseph McCarthy and Roy M. Cohn.

Soros Money Matters

by Jeffrey Steinberg

Aug. 17—The African-American community in the United States today is facing grave challenges and threats. Black unemployment, particularly youth unemployment, is the highest among all identity groups in the nation. Cities across the country are being hit with an epidemic of heroin addiction and deaths, hitting the African-American community above all others. The militarization of local police, accelerated following Sept. 11, 2001, at the initiative of then-Vice President Dick Cheney, who started the program of arming local police with surplus Pentagon equipment when he was Secretary of Defense under George H.W. Bush, has contributed to a skyrocketing number of incidents of police use of excessive force, targeted, most often, against African-American youth.

There is no question that, in many parts of the Southern United States, racism is on the rise and is compounding all of the larger social and economic crises confronting the African-American community.

Since the killing of Treyvon Martin in Florida in February 2012, a national movement has "spontaneously" emerged under the Twitter hashtag #BlackLivesMatter.

In recent months, the movement has received widespread and controversial media coverage for its disruptions of campaign events by two leading Democratic Party presidential candidates, Bernie Sanders and Martin O'Malley.

Recently the group attempted to disrupt a campaign event by Republican candidate Jeb Bush.

The group's tactics of singling out the two most progressive Democratic challengers to Hillary Clinton, both of whom have earned Wall Street's fury for promoting the return to Glass-Steagall bank separation, have raised questions about the group's hidden agenda, integrity, and possible secret backers.

On Jan. 14, 2015, before the start of the presidential campaign season, the *Washington Times*' Kelly Riddell published a fairly in-depth review of the history—and finances—of "Black Lives Matter." Her findings, while not surprising for those who have studied the so-called "color revolutions" in Eastern Europe, North Africa and the Middle East, were dramatic: Billionaire hedge fund speculator and fanatical drug-legalization promoter George Soros has been the biggest single financier of the protest movements that began with the Treyvon Martin killing, and escalated following the police killing of Michael Brown in Ferguson, Missouri on Aug. 14, 2014. Soros-funded groups, including his own Open Society Foundation and Drug Policy Alliance, have poured an estimated $33 million into the cause in recent years.

While the motives of the grass-roots protesters who have been riled up, legitimately, against police brutality and racism, are not in question here, the motives and actions of Soros, who was an early and critically important supporter of Barack Obama's presidential quest, and who is one of the nastiest of the London-trained and sponsored ravenous speculators, can and must be put under a microscope.

The facts, as documented by Riddell and corroborated by public documents filed by the Soros front groups under IRS requirements, are clear. As Riddell described it: "There's a solitary man at the financial center of the Ferguson protest movement. No, it's not

Why are black activists concentrating their attacks on the most progressive Democratic candidates? Here, a protestor from #BlackLivesMatter interrupts Martin O'Malley at the Netroots Convention on July 20, 2015.

victim Michael Brown or Officer Darren Wilson. It's not even the Rev. Al Sharpton, despite his ubiquitous campaign on TV and the streets. Rather, it's liberal billionaire George Soros, who has built a business empire that dominates, across the ocean in Europe, while forging a political machine powered by nonprofit foundations that impact American politics and policy, not unlike what he did with MoveOn.org."

Riddell reported, "In all, Mr. Soros gave at least $33 million in one year to support already-established groups that emboldened the grass-roots, on-the-ground activists in Ferguson, according to the most recent tax filings of his nonprofit Open Society Foundations."

Who Is George Soros?

Soros became a household name in 1992, when his Quantum Fund made a $2 billion killing in just 48 hours, betting on the breakup of the European Rate Mechanism (ERM), a quasi-fixed exchange rate system, regulating currencies among the major European nations. The collapse of the ERM created the preconditions for the launching of Europe's deeply flawed Maastricht single-currency system, a system that is now in the process of disintegrating. While Soros was charged with busting the British Pound Sterling, the reality is that his breaking of the ERM was done on behalf of his patrons in the City of London and the Anglo-Dutch offshore financial havens. Like the British actions in the late 1960s, preceding the end of the Bretton Woods System, Soros' actions served British strategic interests, which were concealed by the temporary hit that the British currency experienced.[1]

The goal of Maastricht, as envisioned by then-British Prime Minister Margaret Thatcher, French President François Mitterrand, and U.S. President George H.W. Bush, was to straight-jacket Germany in continental Western Europe, to prevent any potential future German-Russian economic "Ostpolitik" that could open the door for genuine Eurasian economic cooperation, as has recently emerged with the BRICS New Development Bank and China's "One Belt, One Road" program. Former German Chancellor Helmut Kohl, in his memoirs, acknowleged that he was politically blackmailed by the Thatcher-Mitterrand-Bush combination into accepting the single-currency swindle as a

---

1. 1. See EIR Special Report, "The true story of Soros the Golem: A profile of megaspeculator George Soros,'" April 1977.

Billionaire George Soros, shown here at the Munich Security Conference in 2011, is the moneybags for peaceful and violent upsurges worldwide—from Ferguson, Missouri to Kiev, Ukraine.

creative commons/Harald Dettenborn

precondition for European acceptance of German reunification.

Soros, by his own admission, developed his survival skills as a rapacious speculator, while serving in Nazi-occupied Hungary, as a teenage assistant to a Quisling government official, who confiscated Jewish properties and facilitated the extermination of Jews in the Nazi concentration camps. In interviews with PBS public televion and CBS Sixty Minutes, Soros candidly acknowledged, unapologetically, his wartime experiences and how they shaped his future investment strategies.

The job of Soros' Nazi occupation-regime protector, Mr. Baumbach, by Soros' own account to PBS's Adam Smith, "was to take over Jewish properties, so I actually went with him and we took possession of these large estates. That was my identity. So it's a strange, very strange life. I was 14 years old at the time."

In a family-published autobiography, Soros' father admitted that he fretted over his son George's zealous adaptation to his role as the adopted son of a Nazi official, charged with confiscating Jewish property and sending the owners off to the death camps. George Soros, in contrast, valued the experience as a life-shaping event that taught him that, under crisis conditions, you do whatever is required to survive, regardless of the moral consequences.

Soros Assets Pour into Ferguson

George Soros has devoted his billionaire fortune to two principal causes: drug legalization and radical population reduction. His Open Society Institute has run a program on "Dying in America" for many years, and

Soros has been, for the past quarter-century, the largest single donor to the movement for total drug legalization. Soros took over the Drug Policy Foundation and launched, with his tax-exempt billions of dollars, the Drug Policy Alliance.

This author attended a Drug Policy Foundation convention several years ago, in which Soros representatives promoted the legalization of *all* drugs, including crack cocaine. During that closed-door panel, the Soros speakers lamented the lack of enthusiasm for drug legalization within the African-American community.

Drugs are such a scourge in the African-American communities across the country, that even Soros' money could not buy enough credible promoters of drug legalization to satisfy the billionaire's ambitions.

So, the Soros public relations machine developed sophisticated subterfuges to conceal the total drug legalization agenda. They launched a multi-year campaign for "medical marijuana," dodging the more controversial scheme for pot legalization, until the population had been saturated with propaganda over the virtues of marijuana as a pain reliever and appetite-enhancer for cancer patients.

Soros next launched a multi-million dollar campaign against the incarceration of far-too-many African-American youth for non-violent drug charges. It was this movement for "drug legislation reform" and "decriminalization" that perfectly intersected the Martin and Brown cases.

The Soros Octopus

Soros' flagship Open Society Foundation has spawned dozens of wholly-owned and funded front groups over the years. In the cookie-cutter recipe for "color revolutions," Soros-backed groups come together in "ad hoc alliances" on behalf of specific causes, all of which receive disproportionate volumes of mass media coverage and promotion—often, initially, through Soros-funded social media fronts.

As documented by the *Washington Times*'s Kelly

creative commons

What Soros money wrought in Ukraine: A riot scene in Kiev, February 18, 2014.

Riddell, Soros-funded groups descended on Ferguson, Missouri in droves in the wake of the Michael Brown killing.

"Buses of activists from the Samuel DeWitt Proctor Conference in Chicago; from the Drug Policy Alliance, Make the Road New York and Equal Justice USA from New York; from Sojourners, the Advancement Project and Center for Community Change in Washington; and networks from the Gamaliel Foundation—all funded in part by Mr. Soros—descended on Ferguson starting in August (2014) and later organized protests and gatherings in the city until late last month."

As recounted by Riddell, the key organization, on top of the "coalition," was the Drug Policy Alliance. The group's policy manager Kassandra Frederique, landed in Ferguson in Oct. 2014. "We recognized this movement is similar to the work we're doing at DPA. The war on drugs has always been to operationalize, institutionalize, and criminalize people of color."

Frederique functions, in effect, as a controller of the Black Lives Matter founders, including Opal Tometi, head of the Black Alliance for Just Immigration, a group that got $100,000 from Soros in 2011, the last year for which records are available.

Another Soros-bankrolled group, Race Forward, which publishes the online newsletter Colorlines, covered the convergence on Ferguson of Soros-backed insurgents, and kept the Ferguson situation alive through social media reporting. Colorlines got $200,000 from Soros in 2011 and has shamelessly promoted the #BlackLivesMatter hashtag. Other Soros-bankrolled groups that were present in force in Ferguson, included Organization for Black Struggle (OBS) and Missourians Organizing for Reform and Empowerment (MORE). All told, Soros tax-exempt funds kicked in $5.4 million dollars for Ferguson protests alone in 2014.

Ultimately, the Ferguson protest led to the national media promotion of #BlackLivesMatter, and the formation of an all-Soros funded "coalition" called the "Hands Up Coalition," a reference to the claim that Michael Brown had his hands up when he was shot and killed by police. OBS and MORE formed the backbone of the "Hands Up Coalition," along with yet another Soros-bankrolled group, Dream Defenders. Hands Up Coalition launched a website and dubbed 2015 "The Year of Resistance."

Another of the important Soros-funded groups that fed the Ferguson ferment was the Gamaliel Foundation, a nationwide network of interreligious grass roots protest groups. President Barack Obama worked for Gamaliel Foundation in Chicago at the start of his political career. In addition, the Samuel Dewitt Proctor Conference, which also flooded Ferguson with activists, lists Rev. Jeremiah Wright, President Obama's religious advisor, on its board of trustees. The Conference received $250,000 from Soros foundations in the last available reporting year, 2011.

The Millennial Activists United, a group that has taken the lead in social network propaganda for the Ferguson and related protests that helped launch #BlackLivesMatter as a national media phenonenon, is partnered with the Soros-backed Gamaliel Foundation and the Advancement Project, a group that received $500,000 from Soros in 2013, according to their own website, and which is a training center for "color revolution" activists. The Advancement Project, based in Washington, D.C., arranged a face-to-face meeting between Soros' legions of Ferguson protesters and President Barack Obama in Dec. 2014, to give the White House an inside picture of the network's strategy for exploiting Ferguson into a nationwide movement.

In addition to Opal Tometi of the Black Alliance for Just Immigration, the other two founders of #BlackLivesMatter are Patrisse Cullors and Alicia Garza. Both come out of the Soros-funded stable of organizations. Garza, Cullors, and Tometi reportedly met while all three were working for BOLD (Black Organizing for Leadership & Dignity). Advisory Council chairwoman Alta Starr is a fund-manager for the Ford Founation and the New World Foundation, and an advisor to Soros' Open Society Foundation's Southern Initiative. She is a board member of the National Domestic Workers Alliance, an organization headed by #BlackLivesMatter founder Alicia Garza.

Patrisse Cullors, a Fullbright scholar, is director of the Ella Baker Center for Human Rights, an organization both funded by Soros and founded by Van Jones, who served in the Obama White House as the President's Special Advisor for Green Jobs, Enterprise, and Innovation at the White House Council on Environmental Quality. In 2008, Jones launched Green for All, an effort to sell radical environmentalist schemes in the minority community. Green for All was bankrolled by the Open Society Foundation, and that funding continues to the present. Jones left the Obama White House under a cloud, and is now a senior fellow at the Soros-created and funded Center for American Progress.

'Open System Theory'

Soros' efforts to bankroll and employ the nexus of organizations now grouped under the #BlackLivesMatter umbrella, like his parallel efforts in Ukraine, Georgia and other nations targeted for regime-change "color revolutions," are part of a larger effort to create social movements that can be manipulated and deployed against geo-strategic targets, usually nation-state regimes that do not adapt to the demands of the London-Wall Street financier oligarchy that Soros represents.

As early as the late 1960s, social engineers like the Tavistock Institute's Dr. Frederick Emery wrote of the "hypnotic effects" of mass media, and the future prospects of instantly activating what he called "swarming adolescents" in "rebellious hysteria." In 1971, as part of a UNESCO-funded Tavistock research program, Dr. Emery, along with the Wharton School's Dr. Eric Trist, developed a concept of future mass psychological manipulation that they called "sociotechnical systems" and "Open Systems Theory." Their objective was to conduct real-life mass social manipulations. It was a long-term scheme, which Drs. Emery and Trist summarized in an article published in Tavistock's journal *Human Relations* under the title "Next 30 Years: Concepts, Methods and Anticipations."

Future reports in this series will explore in-depth the larger schemes for mass social manipulation.

Two Weapons Against Thermonuclear War

The following discussion occurred on the weekly LaRouche PAC webcast on August 14. The video is available for viewing.

Jason Ross: Good evening. This is Aug. 14, 2015, and you're watching the regularly-scheduled Friday night webcast here at LaRouche PAC. My name is Jason Ross, and I'm joined in the studio tonight by Megan Beets and Benjamin Deniston of the LaRouche PAC Science Research Team, and by Jeff Steinberg of *Executive Intelligence Review*.

We had a significant discussion with Mr. LaRouche and Mrs. LaRouche earlier today about the topics that we'll be discussing tonight. The first topic we're going to take up is Obama and the 25th Amendment. The 25th Amendment to the U.S. Constitution was adopted in 1967, in the aftermath of some of the uncertainty about succession that was revealed after the Kennedy assassination. One aspect of this Amendment, Section Four, entails the operation of the Executive Branch to remove an incapacitated President.

Now, any person who believes nuclear war is a potentially sensible policy, or believes nuclear war is winnable or even survivable, is clearly insane—and therefore a likely target for the use of the 25th Amendment. I'd like to ask Jeff Steinberg to start us off this evening, discussing the importance of the 25th Amendment with regards to Obama, particularly in light of the Congress being out of session at the moment.

White House/Pete Souza

From the moment he entered the Oval Office, President Obama pursued a policy of confrontation with Russian President Vladimir Putin. Here, their first meeting at Putin's dacha outside Moscow, July 7, 2009.

The 25th Amendment: The Precedents

Jeff Steinberg: Thanks, Jason. As Jason said, the 25th Amendment was drafted in 1965 by Senator Birch Bayh and Congressman Emmanuel Celler. It passed both Houses of Congress, and over the course of a two-year period and was ratified by the initially required 39 states. So, this is a relatively new development, and it was indeed provoked by the fact that there was tremendous uncertainty around the Kennedy assassination; largely over the question of what if President Kennedy had survived the assassination attempt, but was physically or mentally completely incapacitated.

This was something that was considered very seriously. There were earlier efforts in the 1960s to take this question up, right after Kennedy was killed; but eventually the Amendment was passed. Now, this is not something that is unprecedented; in fact, in the period following the formal ratification, the 25th Amendment was put into play on at least three occasions.

Nixon

First of all, during the final days of President Richard Nixon, when there was grave uncertainty about Nixon's mental stability. There was tremendous fear that he might order some kind of military action; whether a domestic coup-type action, or possibly instigating a war in order to hold on, to really to cling to his office. And at that time, the 25th Amendment was in play.

A number of members of the Nixon Cabinet, and the White House Chief of Staff, who at the time was Gen. Alexander Haig; you had Henry Kissinger in the dual role of National Security Advisor and Secretary of State. And you had James Rodney Schlesinger as Secretary of Defense. So, members of the Cabinet, under the terms of the 25th Amendment, were gauging whether or not Nixon—in his potential insanity—posed a dire threat to the national security of the United States and the world.

We have accounts directly from Schlesinger that he informed the Chairman of the Joint Chiefs of Staff that if Nixon issued military orders, the Chiefs were not to implement them without first clearing it, with Schlesinger and other members of the Cabinet. That was not some kind of rogue action; it was an invoking of the 25th Amendment.

In fact, Nixon was presented with three options by leading members of his own party. He was presented with the option number one of facing certain impeachment, in the United States Senate. Sen. Howard Baker was one of the people, who directly went to Nixon and told him that there were enough Republican votes along with Democratic votes, that if he went to trial in the U.S. Senate, he would be impeached and convicted. The

Then-Secretary of Defense James Schlesinger invoked the 25th Amendment against Nixon. Here, he confers with fellow-cabinet member, NSC advisor and Secretary of State Henry Kissinger.

second option was, of course, resignation; but the third option that was also there, was that if Nixon tried to take some kind of irrational action, the Cabinet was prepared to invoke the 25th Amendment; immediately remove him from office, and install Vice President Gerald Ford as the acting President.

Now, here we are in August of 2015; Congress is scattered all over the country and probably around the world. And so, we have a situation in which the danger, the imminent danger of a war provocation coming out of President Obama is such that it is incumbent on members of the Cabinet to carefully gauge his state of mind, and seriously put in play, the option of invoking the 25th Amendment.

As Jason said a few moments ago, what could be more insane than even contemplating provoking a war against Russia, knowing full well that Russia is prepared to retaliate with a massive second strike? Russia presently has an arsenal of 4,000 active and mothballed nuclear weapons. So, this would be a war of annihilation. Nothing is more mad than that kind of consideration; and we're very, very close to that. We'll pick up that theme a bit later in this broadcast.

Reagan

Now, you also had two instances with President Ronald Reagan, where there was consideration of the 25th Amendment. Obviously, the first occasion was in 1981, when Reagan was the target of an assassination attempt by Bush family friend John Hinckley. And at that time, Reagan was seriously injured, and there was an immediate question about whether or not he would sufficiently recover, to be able to resume his duties as President. Fortunately, he did recover, and so that issue was resolved, happily for the country and the world.

But in the mid-1980s, after the Iran-Contra Affair came to light, there was again movement, principally coming from the Bush circles, within the Administration, to claim that Reagan was no longer mentally fit to be President. Once again, former Sen. Howard Baker played a pivotal role in assessing the 25th Amendment's relevance. Baker had been appointed White House Chief of Staff, to clean up some of the mess that had been left by people like George Bush and Ollie North in the Iran-Contra Affair.

Baker recounted to several journalists soon afterwards, that he was told by members of the Reagan Cabinet—presumably also by Vice President Bush—that his first assignment on coming in as White House Chief of Staff was to evaluate and provide an assessment to the Cabinet, on whether President Reagan could still serve as President, or whether he was showing signs of diminished mental functioning.

And Baker reported that he was extraordinarily nervous, going into the first Cabinet meeting after he assumed the Chief of Staff post. He knew that he had to make a kind of evaluation on the spot of Reagan's competence to continue to serve as President. He said Reagan walked into the room, sat down, and immediately cracked four or five very, very funny jokes, and Howard Baker breathed a sigh of relief that President Reagan had all of his marbles, and the issue was settled.

But the question right now is one of immediate urgency, because we could be hours, we could be days, we could be weeks away from an incident provoking a war which President Obama would readily and happily launch a nuclear attack against Russia, knowing full well that could be the trigger for a war of annihilation. So, the 25th Amendment has to be something that is being seriously considered by members of the Obama Cabinet. And it's important for you, leading citizens of this republic, to be aware of, and to also come to grips with and face the reality of, precisely the kind of moment of danger that we're living through right now.

Reagan Presidential Library

The assassination attempt against President Ronald Reagan was only one of the occasions for considering the application of the 25th Amendment.

2. 'Unsurvivable'

Benjamin Deniston: So, I'm going to be posing the second question, but I would like to first stick on this same point that Jason introduced and Jeff just raised. Any world leader who by his actions is effectively threatening the use of thermonuclear weapons in an offensive manner, is mentally unfit to serve in office.

Now, the LaRouche PAC in 2012 treated this subject in a documentary produced under the direction of Lyndon LaRouche; a 35-minute feature documentary entitled, "Unsurvivable." And today, given the events that we are now living through, and fighting on right now, today, this week, this month, we highly recommend that our viewers watch, if you haven't watched it before; or if you've seen it, re-watch, this feature 2012 production by LaRouche PAC—"Unsurvivable." We've posted a link to the video in the description of this current broadcast today, so you can access it right there. But we highly recommend that you watch it, watch it again; circulate it.

This documentary provides a rather unnerving, but completely realistic, completely accurate, account of how quickly a thermonuclear war could break out and end civilization as we know it. And how close we've actually come, in 2012 and again today, to that horrific reality under the policies of Obama.

How many Americans actually know, have a real sense of, the level of thermonuclear firepower that has right now been placed into Obama's hands? And how quickly that could be deployed?

For example, as we covered in this video, over something around half of the United States' active inventory of thermonuclear warheads is currently being carried on a fleet of Ohio-class submarines. Now, each of these submarines is capable alone of deploying 24 Trident missiles. Each single missile can carry up to 8 individual thermonuclear warheads; 8 individual, distinct thermonuclear bombs—explosive devices—deployed from that one missile. So, if you take 24 missiles, 8 warheads per missile, that is a capacity of nearly 200 thermonuclear bombs, explosives, per submarine.

Now, each warhead, once released from its missile,

U.S. Navy/Rex Nelson

One single Ohio-class ballistic-missile submarine, like this USS Alaska, can carry the firepower to destroy up to 200 major cities in a matter of minutes.

upon the reentry process, can be directed to an individual, distinct target. And each warhead, depending on the size of device chosen for that warhead, can be somewhere between 6 and 30 times more powerful than the atomic bomb dropped on Hiroshima at the end of World War II.

So, just to give you a sense, that's the power of thermonuclear weapons, thermonuclear war. *One single submarine*—one submarine can carry the firepower to destroy up to 200 major cities in a matter of minutes. Now, I would ask our audience if you can even name 200 major cities off the top of your head. Two hundred major cities, containing potentially hundreds of millions of people, at the mercy of the firepower contained in just one of these submarines.

Now, with 14 of these submarines as part of our nuclear capability in our Navy fleet, the total potential capacity is in the thousands of thermonuclear warheads. And as we covered in the video, all of this can be released in a matter of seconds. And with the ability to secretly position these submarines off the coast of a target nation, it could take less than 10 minutes—a matter of minutes—for the warheads to actually reach their targets.

Obviously, any attempt to make such a strike, would insure an immediate retaliatory strike; and the total effects would not just destroy the targeted sites. It wouldn't just destroy the military targets, or the cities, or the infrastructure targeted directly by the weapons;

but it would have catastrophic effects on the Earth's atmosphere, the climate system, creating what's been referred to as a nuclear winter effect, which would last years. So, this is truly a global catastrophe.

Now, this is just a taste of the capability that we're currently leaving right now in the hands of Barack Obama. And I think it's appropriate to highlight one of the closing points of emphasis in this 2012 LaRouche PAC documentary, "Unsurvivable." In August 1983, almost 32 years ago to the day, the third in a series of international seminars, dedicated to addressing and removing the threat of thermonuclear war was held in Erice, Italy. The subject of that 1983 conference was "The Technical Basis for Peace." And that particular conference featured discussions of LaRouche's SDI program, including contributions from Dr. Edward Teller on the United States side, from Dr. Evgeny Velikhov from Russia, among many other leading figures.

But what was interesting was that the conference chairman, Antonino Zichichi, during his commencement address to that conference, noted very clearly that the threat of thermonuclear war doesn't simply come from the weapons themselves; but also, he emphasized the danger from the personalities of individuals who could come into a position of power where they would have the ability to deploy this potentially civilization-ending capability.

Just to read a small quote from Zichichi on this; he said: "In history fools have never been lacking.... Sooner or later—in 10, 20, or maybe 100 years—a fool will come forth. When the fool appears on the scene, mankind will find itself with hundreds of millions of dead, with the ozone layer destroyed by 50%, with the average temperature of the planet lowered by at least 7 degrees, with an enormous amount of radioactivity, and with mountains of ashes instead of the vast treasures accumulated in centuries of laborious and intelligent activity, in all parts of the world."

Now, that was stated 32 years ago, almost to the day; and now we find ourselves here now, for nearly seven years, the United States has been under the direction of just such a fool—Barack Obama.

Ukrainian Nazis: Trigger for Nuclear War

Now, in our discussions with Mr. LaRouche earlier today, he strongly emphasized that Mr. Obama's regime-change operation in Ukraine is a leading flashpoint which could start thermonuclear war. Obama's coup in Ukraine, which has created a military conflict directly on Russia's border, with Obama-backed, Nazi paramilitary groups, including the Right Sector, driving this conflict. Mr. LaRouche said, "This is Obama's Nazi policy in Ukraine. Obama's policies come with swastikas." And LaRouche emphasized that people have to take a look at the global strategic—and not just local—significance of this Obama-backed Nazi Right Sector operation in Ukraine.

So Jeff, we were discussing this with Mr. LaRouche this morning; and we are hoping you could provide an elaboration of Mr. LaRouche's remarks on the significance of this Ukraine operation as understood from this standpoint.

Steinberg: We've been warning on this broadcast for weeks now, that the gravest danger of a provocation leading to war, is in the immediate period that we're in right now, namely August, with the U.S. Congress out of session, and with the Joint Chiefs of Staff and other military institutions going through a major personnel transition. In our discussion earlier today, we reviewed the fact that over the course of this Summer, and going into the Fall, there has been a continuous series of NATO maneuvers in the area immediately adjacent to Russia: in the Black Sea region, in the Baltic Sea region, in other parts of Eastern and Southern Europe. In fact, there are major maneuvers that begin mid-September and will run through November—the largest NATO maneuvers directed at Russia, since the end of the Cold War.

Mr. LaRouche's point was that the danger is more immediate. If you look at September, October, November, you're perhaps missing the most obvious and most dangerous trigger: namely, the fact that the Victoria Nuland's Right Sector apparatus, is preparing an immediate second Maidan coup inside Kiev, with the objective of completely ripping up the Minsk accords, and

At the August 1983 Erice Conference, Conference Chairman Antonino Zichichi warned: "Sooner or later... a fool will come forth," and "mankind will find itself with hundreds of millions of dead, with the ozone layer destroyed by 50%, with the average temperature of the planet lowered by at least 7 degrees, with an enormous amount of radioactivity, and with mountains of ashes instead of the vast treasures accumulated in centuries of laborious and intelligent activity, in all parts of the world."

CC/Gabriella Clare Marino
Professor Antonino Zichichi

launching an immediate war against Russian-backed elements in Eastern Ukraine.

Now the Speaker of the Russian Duma, earlier this week, issued a very direct warning, echoing what Mr. LaRouche has been saying for weeks now. Namely, that we are facing an August war-provocation crisis, centered around Ukraine, but with the potential to immediately break out of any bounds of control.

We've talked in earlier broadcasts about the fact that the world was very fortunate back in 1962, at the time of the Cuban Missile Crisis, that there was already an ongoing, very personal and very cordial but tough dialogue underway between President John F. Kennedy and Soviet Premier Nikita Khrushchov, because they were both concerned that they might one day be facing the horrible moment of decision, whether to order the use of nuclear weapons, and face the possible annihilation of mankind. Because that dialogue had been going on, for quite some time, for almost two years prior to the Cuban Missile Crisis, there was a meeting of the minds. An agreement could be worked out, despite the fact that many key advisors, both to Kennedy and Khrushchov, were arguing for confrontation.

There is no such personal rapport between President Obama, and Russian President Putin. If anything, President Obama has represented a provocation, a confrontation against Russia, against President Putin, at every turn. It began from the time of their very first meeting in 2009.

Now, where are we at this moment?

As I said, the Right Sector is on a rampage. In fact, an article that appears today in *The National Interest*, a widely-read online national security journal here in Washington, provides a very pointed warning. The real threat coming from Ukraine is not in the East, is not in

---

LaRouche warned: "If you look at September, October, November, you're perhaps missing the most obvious and most dangerous trigger: namely, the fact that Victoria Nuland's Right Sector apparatus, is preparing an immediate second Maidan coup inside Kiev, with the objective of completely ripping up the Minsk accords, and launching an immediate war against Russian-backed elements in Eastern Ukraine."

---

the immediate issue, of the confrontation around the Eastern Republics bordering on Russia. The real danger, the real threat, is coming from Western Ukraine, which is the base of operation, of the Right Sector. These are outright Nazis. Their pedigree we have documented time and time again. These are the second and third generation followers of Stepan Bandera, who was an outright Nazi collaborator with Hitler during the Second World War, who carried out genocide against the populations of the Soviet Union, Poland, and other countries in the area.

And the fact of the matter is, that those networks were saved and protected by British and American intelligence in the early days of the Cold War. They were given protection; they were given financing; they nurtured second and third generations. And now what we see in the Right Sector, in the Azov Brigade and other military formations that are outright neo-Nazis, is the immediate danger and hair-trigger of war.

This is not something that happened organically. You had Victoria Nuland, the Assistant U.S. Secretary of State for European and Eurasian Affairs, openly flaunting the fact that the United States was backing these literal Nazis. The Obama Administration was backing a Nazi coup in Ukraine. Most of the American and European media have blacked this out, but the reality is unmistakable. And this is where you've got a potential immediate trigger for war.

Russians Deliver Some Warnings

The Russians have not only issued warnings about the Guns of August, but they've been taking a number of measures aimed at delivering an *unmistakable* message to Washington, and to European NATO capitals, that Russia has an unstoppable, second-strike retaliatory capability. Over the course of the Summer, you've had incidents in July where Russian strategic bombers, the Bear bombers, were flying directly off the coast of California. Where for periods of weeks at a time, Russian equivalents of the Ohio-class submarines, carrying nuclear weapons, potentially, were operating in waters of the Caribbean and right off Gulf of Mexico.

So, make no mistake about it. If an incident kicks off inside Ukraine, and leads to the kind of escalation where the arsenal of tactical nuclear weapons that the United States has deployed all over Eastern Europe, is used, Russia will respond with a massive retaliation that they're absolutely capable of carrying out. And we will be facing an absolute condition of potential human annihilation.

This is the specter that we're dealing with. This is what happens when someone is allowed into the Presidency of the United States, who's incapable of comprehending the awesome responsibility and the absolute danger represented by a conflict between the United States and Russia. And this is something here and now. It could happen tomorrow morning. It could happen a week from now. It could happen in early September. But we are in the zone, right now, with Congress out of town, spread out all across the United States; with no center of opposition as we saw in September of 2013, when the Joint Chiefs of Staff and others intervened forcefully to prevent the start of a U.S. bombing campaign against the Assad government in Syria, that would have, in all likelihood, led to an ISIS government being installed over the totality of Syria by now.

So, this is the reality.

Now, just to put a further punctuation on the point that Ben just made, about the 35 minute video-documentary, which all of you should really take the time to watch, or re-watch, right now: The fact of the matter is, when that "Unsurvivable" video was made public, we received a number of messages of gratitude from people directly involved in the strategic nuclear program of the United States government. They said: You've presented in a concise and highly accurate fashion, the reality that we live with every moment of every day. And it's essential that the American people realize that the time-

Here we can see "Azov" and there is even a swastika.

youtube

The Azov Battalion underscores LaRouche's point: "This is Obama's Nazi policy in Ukraine. Obama's policies come with swastikas."

frame for making a decision, on whether or not to launch a nuclear strike, or launch a retaliatory strike based on the apparent launching of a first strike, is reduced to a matter of minutes.

And as Mr. LaRouche has warned, the totality of a thermonuclear exchange, a nuclear war on a global scale, will be over in a matter of hours, but the consequences may never be reversible.

3. Empire Rails Against Sanity

Ross: Let's take our institutional question of the evening: Tony Blair followed up his earlier denunciation of [candidate for head of the British Labour Party] Jeremy Corbyn and his supporters with an impassioned letter just printed in the *Guardian*. In his letter, Blair says the Labour Party risks "annihilation," according to him, if Jeremy Corbyn wins the party's leadership contest, and that the party was walking "over the cliff's edge," in his words.

And his comments come as another Labour Party leader candidate, Yvette Cooper, is set to criticize Corbyn as not having "credible policies."

So the question that came in to Mr. LaRouche was, "In your view, is Mr. Corbyn qualified to be the Labour Party's next leader?"

Steinberg: I brought some notes from that discussion, because I want to be very precise in terms of what Mr. LaRouche had to say on this.

First of all, the policies that Tony Blair and Yvette Cooper are criticizing, as being the annihilation of the Labour Party, start with the fact that Jeremy Corbyn has said that one of his first priorities, in coming into office would be a full-blown Glass-Steagall policy for Britain: in other words, a total bank separation. The Bank of England, the House of Lords, have adopted a policy that's a kind of halfway measure that they call "ring-fencing," and the later version was "electrified ring-fencing." It doesn't really break up the banks; it doesn't do what is required.

And so, Corbyn has said that the first order of business will be exactly to do that.

There's a very clear parallel between the fact that Martin O'Malley, one of the Democratic candidates for President, has said the very same thing: that Glass-Steagall is the defining issue for the 2016 Presidential elections. And because of that, O'Malley has been declared public enemy number one by Wall Street. And so, when Tony Blair speaks, the City of London is flapping his jaws. What you're dealing with here is a policy that would really represent the annihilation of those in the financial establishment, particularly those aligned with the British Monarchy, who want to keep the British people suppressed, looted, bankrupted, ignorant, for the sake of bailing out a bankrupt financial system.

Now, what Mr. LaRouche said is that England is a very class-conscious place, and the privileged layers of society want to protect their own interests. Well, the situation has reached the point where unless you're prepared to sustain the whole of the people of the United Kingdom, which is not just England, but includes Scotland—which is obviously in a very restive mood right now, virtually in a state of secession from the United Kingdom; what happens in Scotland clearly spills over into Ireland and Wales.

So, you have a situation where what's urgently required is the principle of equity, where the interests of the common man and common woman of England, are clearly put in the category of priorities.

Right now the British system doesn't supply this kind of assistance, and this kind of policy, to benefit all. Average households need this kind of equitable protection, and this is a primary responsibility of government, to assure these kinds of equitable arrangements. In effect, Corbyn is proposing those kinds of policies, and therefore is eminently qualified to be able to actually take over charge of the Labour Party, and go beyond that to perhaps become, in the very near future, a Prime Minister.

Now, ballots for the Labour Party vote have gone out starting today, and the voting will take place, and will be completed by the 10th of September, and the results will be announced two days later. Right now, Corbyn is polling about 54% against three other candidates. So, we'll see what comes out of that.

Mr. LaRouche went further. He said, look, you've got other problems that are coming up in the British situation. You have a British Monarchy that is entering into a very, very clear and obvious senility factor, both Queen Elizabeth II and Prince Philip. You've got a stupefied monarchy, and don't kid yourself: the monarchy is the real center of power in Britain, and in the entire Commonwealth of nations, the 53 countries that are under the overall British Commonwealth umbrella.

So, vigorous reform is urgently needed. There's a brawl underway inside the Royal Family. We've discussed this in several recent shows. There is a move to dump the monarchy system altogether. And one of the weapons that's being used by proponents of this policy, is widespread exposure of the Nazi history of the British Royal Family, the House of Windsor.

What LaRouche said is: the Corbyn option, an equitable approach to the economics of the entirety of the United Kingdom, and take the senility factor out of the monarchy, in fact, dump the monarchy altogether; and this can be not only a very positive development from the standpoint of Britain, but can have a dramatic effect in Europe as a whole, where Britain is trying to renegotiate its entire relationship with the European Union. And where we saw, in August of 2013, that when the

creative commons/Jason

Jeremy Corbyn, shown here at an anti-austerity rally in London July 8, 2015, has proposed policies of equity for all Britons, and "is eminently qualified to be able to actually take over charge of the Labour Party...."

British Parliament refused to go along with the idea of a war to overthrow the Assad government in Syria, the U.S. Congress felt a lot more comfortable resisting Obama, and, in fact, succeeded in stopping that war from happening.

4. Hillary Clinton: Tell the Truth about Benghazi

Megan Beets: So to bring things back to the situation in the United States: on July 28, LaRouche PAC released a mass circulation statement, entitled, "Hillary Clinton Must Tell the Truth about Benghazi, and Bring Down Obama Before He Unleashes the Guns of August." The statement has gained circulation nationwide.

The statement underscores the critical role that Hillary Clinton uniquely can and must play in getting President Obama's finger off the thermonuclear button, by telling the truth about what she knows actually happened on the evening of Sept. 11, 2012 in Benghazi, Libya; what she knows about the President's role in lying to cover up what actually happened; and in his ordering Hillary to lie as well, to cover up his crimes, which she did.

While coming clean in this way would obviously end Hillary's chances of becoming President, it's a very small price to pay to pull civilization back from the brink of thermonuclear war.

Given what has already been discussed this evening, regarding just how close civilization is to total annihilation if Obama is allowed to remain in office, in a moment I'd like to ask Jeff to come to the podium to address the situation inside the United States, around the process of the formation of a new Presidency.

The Democratic National Committee, for example, on behalf of Obama, is doing everything it can to shut down any debate or discussion of these kinds of issues during the campaign process, and to very rapidly "crown" Hillary the nominee, as long as she keeps her mouth shut. Now, Hillary's role in this Presidential process is critical, but, in the way that we've outlined it, even if it's not exactly the role she envisioned for herself in the Presidency.

So, Jeff, given that situation, and also looking more broadly at the long-term destruction of the U.S., at the complete corruption within the leadership of both parties, what must we deal with, in order to bring about a viable new Presidency?

CSPAN

"Hillary Clinton has it within her power to step forward now—not in October when she's scheduled, to testify under oath before the Select Committee on Benghazi—but right now, tomorrow morning, call a press conference, and just simply tell the American people what she knows, about President Obama's lying about Benghazi." Here, Clinton at the January 23, 2013 Senate hearing on the subject.

Obama Supports Terrorists

Steinberg: Hillary Clinton is in possession of the second shoe, that could be brought down on President Obama. We discussed earlier in this show the prospect of the 25th Amendment, which puts an enormous amount of onus, on members of the Cabinet and the White House staff, to face the reality that you have a very dangerous man sitting in the Oval Office, who could make a decision that leads to the annihilation of mankind.

Hillary Clinton has it within *her* power to step forward now—not in October when she's scheduled, to testify under oath before the Select Committee on Benghazi—but *right now*, tomorrow morning, call a press conference, and just simply tell the American people what she knows, about President Obama's lying about Benghazi. If you put what Hillary Clinton knows, and *must say publicly*, in the first person, together with what came out in the past week from Gen. Michael Flynn, the former head of the Defense Intelligence Agency, you have a crushing indictment of President Obama.

What Flynn told Al Jazeera TV, in a 45 minute interview that was aired last week, is that he warned President Obama and others in the cabinet, in August of 2012, that if they persisted in continuing to provide arms to the so-called "Syrian rebels"—and a lot of that arms smuggling was going on out of Benghazi, Libya, that this

would lead to the establishment, of an "Islamic Caliphate" a terrorist hub right on the eastern Mediterranean.

In the interview with Al Jazeera, General Flynn was asked: Well, what you're saying is that President Obama ignored the warnings?

And General Flynn said: No, I did say that, it was worse than that. The warnings were well-received. They were clear, they were concise. And the President decided willfully to go ahead with the policy of arming the Syrian rebels, in spite of the fact that he was accurately told what the consequences would be. (See accompanying article.)

This is the same President who, at 10 o'clock at night on Sept. 11, 2012, ordered Hillary Clinton to lie to the American people, to put out a false press release, talking about a video slandering the Prophet Muhammed, a spontaneous protest demonstration, none of which happened. And this was *fully known* by Secretary Clinton, by President Obama, and by all of the national security officials of the Administration at the time. So this is something that Hillary Clinton considers to be an albatross hanging around her neck, but in reality, it is a weapon, that must be invoked, right now, to get this President out of office.

We have the 25th Amendment ready to be enacted, ready to be activated, and we have Hillary Clinton with the responsibility to the American people and the world, to tell the truth about what she knows.

Options for Survival

Now, it so happens that this has been a very, very bad week, for Secretary Clinton, in her quest for the Democratic Party nomination. Many of you are undoubtedly

---

So now, more than ever, is the moment for the betterment of mankind, to bring an end to the danger of nuclear war, to bring this President down. And she's in a position to exactly that.

---

following the details of the allegations that her private e-mail server that she used in her four years as Secretary of State contained classified material, and that this is a crime. And so, you've got two tracks of attacks, coming down on Hillary Clinton right now. One, very obviously, is coming from the Republicans, as one would expect.

But, the other line of attack, probably the more

deadly line of attack, is coming from people inside the Obama White House itself; whether President Obama is personally involved in this is irrelevant. Valerie Jarrett, Michelle Obama, Susan Rice, all of these top people, the people who have been the inner circle advisors, to President Obama from Day One, are running an operation in tandem with the Republicans, to sink Hillary Clinton. They're floating the name of Vice President Joe Biden, as the Wall Street-acceptable alternative to Hillary Clinton, because Hillary has come out openly saying that she does not support the idea that Glass-Steagall needs to be reinstated, when in fact, that's exactly what must be done.

So you've got the White House, once again—no surprise to us—teaming up with the Republicans, in a nasty political operation. Jarrett, Michelle Obama, the people at the White House don't trust Hillary Clinton. They know that Hillary Clinton has it in her capacity, to tell the truth about Benghazi and bring down President Obama, and they are not confident that she won't do exactly that.

So all the more reason for Hillary to step forward and tell the truth, *right now*. You've already got the knives out against her, not just from the Republicans, but directly from the people who've been her enemies since the time of the 2008 Democratic primaries, who now happen to reside at the White House. Why would Hillary Clinton go *one inch* out of her way, to protect people who are her avowed, deadly enemies?

So now, more than ever, is the moment for the betterment of mankind, to bring an end to the danger of nuclear war, to bring this President down. And she's in a position to exactly that.

Ultimately, President Obama is a stooge for the British Empire, for a faction of the British Empire that is so desperate over their imminent loss of power, between the collapse of the trans-Atlantic financial system and the mental disintegration of the British Monarchy, that they're desperate. But, their desperation is irrelevant if Obama is removed from office. If you no longer have the President of the United States, with his finger on the nuclear button, under British control, the war danger is greatly reduced, virtually eliminated.

So we have two options on the table: The 25th Amendment can be invoked by a select group of members of the current Cabinet, along with the Vice President. And, Hillary Clinton, on her own, can bring about the circumstances where the danger of thermonuclear annihilation is eliminated: There's no reason in the world why she does not do that immediately.

Gen. Michael Flynn, Benghazi, and Why Obama Must Be Removed

by Michele and Jeffrey Steinberg

August 16—In an interview aired on July 31 with Al-Jazeera's program, Head to Head, Lt. General Michael Flynn, the former head of the Defense Intelligence Agency (DIA), made an unprecedented, blunt accusation that the rise of the Islamic State (ISIS) was the result of a "willful decision,"—not an intelligence failure—by the Obama Administration.

The Flynn revelations put even more pressure on former Secretary of State Hillary Clinton to "come clean" on what she personally knows about President Barack Obama's "willful" lying cover-up of the al-Qaeda attack in Benghazi on Sept. 11, 2012, in which U.S. Ambassador Christopher Stevens and three other American officials were killed. The issue on the table, now, with the Flynn revelations on top of the ongoing Benghazi probe by a Congressional select committee is: When will President Obama be held accountable for his lying to the American people? When will he be forced out of office?

Speaking to Mehdi Hasan, the host of "Head to Head," Flynn went further than any other recently retired U.S. military official in condemning the policies of President Barack Obama. Flynn did so, not only in highlighting the August 2012 DIA report (only released to the public in May 2015) that warned the Obama Administration about the rise of the "Islamic State," and the creation of a "caliphate" by Syria-based Islamists and al-Qaeda,—but also in identifying that arms shipments in Libya that had gone to jihadist "allies" of the United States and NATO in the overthrowing of Col. Muammar Qaddafi, were shipped to Syria and became the arsenal that allowed the Islamic State of Iraq and Syria (ISIS), and other jihadist rebels to grow.

Questioned by Hasan, Flynn directly accused the Obama Administration of making a "willful decision" to back the jihadis:

Hasan: You are basically saying that even in government at the time you knew these groups were around, you saw this analysis, and you

Jabhat al-Nusra, one of the jihadist groups the Obama Administration made a "willful decision" to support in Southwest Asia.

were arguing against it, but who wasn't listening?

Flynn: I think the Administration.

Hasan: So the Administration turned a blind eye to your analysis?

Flynn: I don't know that they turned a blind eye, I think it was a decision. I think it was a willful decision.

Hasan: A willful decision to support an insurgency that had Salafists, al-Qaeda and the Muslim Brotherhood?

Flynn: It was a willful decision to do what they're doing.

Later in the interview, Hasan brought up arms flows to the rebels. Another DIA memo from October 2012, released in May 2015 through a Freedom of Information Act lawsuit brought by Judicial Watch, detailed the flow of weapons, grabbed from Qaddafi's vast arsenal, from Benghazi to two Syrian ports under the control of Syrian rebel groups.

Hasan: In 2012 the U.S. was helping coordinate arms transfers to those same groups [Salafists, Muslim Brotherhood, al-Qaeda in Iraq], why did you not stop that if you're worried about the rise of quote-unquote Islamic extremists?

Flynn: I hate to say it's not my job ... but that ... my job was to ... was to ensure that the accuracy of our intelligence that was being presented was as good as it could be.

In effect, Gen. Flynn confirmed that the United States was fully aware of weapons trafficking between Benghazi and Syrian jihadists, but either allowed it to happen, or actively participated in the trafficking. President Obama, in mid-2011, had already stated that U.S. policy was for the Assad government to be overthrown.

What Were the DIA Reports?

When the watchdog group Judicial Watch received a series of reports through Freedom of Information Act lawsuits (FOIA) in May 2015 that forecast the creation of an Islamist caliphate that would target Mosul and Ramadi in Iraq (among other sites in Syria), the State Department, the Administration, and various media outlets—especially those friendly to the White House—trashed the reports as insignificant, unreliable, and virtually unknown. That was a lie. In addition, less publicized FOIA releases of the DIA reports to Judicial Watch in the May 2015 timeframe, show that a ratline of weapons traffic was going directly from the U.S.-installed jihadists in Libya to Syria. Again, the Administration lied and dismissed the reports as insignificant.

But with the on-the-record remarks by Gen. Flynn about how the DIA's warnings about the impending "caliphate" were dismissed because of a "willful decision," these reports are placed in a context that shows that Barack Obama has compromised U.S. National Security with his support for Islamist extremism, including the Muslim Brotherhood. Futhermore, according to years-long investigations by *EIR*, these reports are merely the tip of the iceberg. They should open the door to a full investigation of Obama's pro-Islamist regime-change policy that overthrew Qaddafi and led to the travesty in Libya that killed Ambassador Chris Stevens and three other Americans on September, 11, 2012. It was the same regime-change policy supporting the Islamists, nurtured by the Kingdoms of Britain and Saudi Arabia, which was behind Obama's declaration that Syria's elected President Bashar al Assad should be removed.

Another of the FOIA-released DIA documents from Sept. 16, 2012, provides a detailed account of the premeditated nature of the 9/11/12 attack in Benghazi, saying it was planned for ten days, detailing the groups involved, etc. This further buttresses the case that Obama committed impeachable crimes by falsifying what was a major terrorist attack against a U.S. target on the anniversary of 9/11, and lied to cover it up.

Building the Case for Obama's Impeachment

U.S. intelligence community (USIC) sources have emphasized that the release of the DIA documents, combined with the Flynn interview to Al-Jazeera, represent a clear statement that segments of the Pentagon and USIC believe that President Obama has committed clear impeachable crimes against the U.S. Constitution. They point out that the DIA could have stalled the release of the damning documents, by invoking various security considerations. Instead, the documents were released, making the clear case that the Obama Administration had willfully carried out a policy that gave material support to terrorist organizations, despite clear warnings from official U.S. agencies that the policies would severely jeopardize U.S. and allied national security.

Taken together, the DIA documents made clear that: The Obama Administration proceeded ahead with support for anti-Assad forces, knowing full well that the

The Lebanese Army captured this ship full of arms being sent from Libya to Syrian jihadists in April 2012. As documented in EIR's "Obama's War on America: 9/11 Two," there is considerable evidence those arms came with the blessings of the Obama Administration.

policies would lead to the creation of a terrorist haven, "a jihadist caliphate" on the border region of Iraq and Syria; that the very groups receiving support from the Obama White House, had carried out the premeditated terrorist attacks on the U.S. mission in Benghazi on Sept. 11, 2012, resulting in the murder of Ambassador Chris Stevens and three other American officials; and that the United States continued to sanction arms trafficking to the al-Qaeda-linked Syrian rebels even after the 9/11/12 attacks. Furthermore, President Obama knew full well that the Benghazi attacks were pre-planned, pre-meditated and heavily armed attacks, carried out by al-Qaeda, in revenge for the killing of a top al-Qaeda leader of Libyan descent, and on the anniversary of the original Sept. 11, 2001 attacks.

In effect, the DIA reports fully corroborate what Hillary Clinton personally knows about the lying cover-up ordered by President Obama, to hide the essential facts of the Benghazi attacks, to secure his re-election in the Nov. 2012 presidential vote.

General Flynn Speaks Out

The major U.S. media, for the most part, blocked out the significance of the May 2015 DIA documents' release, compounding the earlier crimes by allowing Obama to continue pursuing the same Syria "regime change" policies, without being held accountable. Had the truth been widely exposed back in May, President

Obama would never have dared to issue his early August order for U.S. forces to attack Syrian government forces if they interfered with the American "vetted, trained and armed" forces. Now, the so-called U.S. approved Division 30 Syrian rebel group has formally announced its alliance with the Nusra Front, the formal al-Qaeda affiliate in Syria.

It is against this backdrop that Gen. Flynn gave his interview to Al-Jazeera on July 29. Gen. Flynn has vast experience in the Middle East and in the war against al-Qaeda and the Islamic State. Before being named head of the Defense Intelligence Agency in April 2014, Gen. Flynn served as Director of Intelligence for the Joint Staff, as Director of Intelligence for the U.S. Central Command, and as Director of Intelligence for the Joint Special Operations Command. In September 2011, immediately prior to being nominated to head the DIA, Gen. Flynn was assigned to the Office of the Director of National Intelligence, as liaison to the international intelligence community.

Gen. Flynn earned the wrath of key Obama advisors at the White House in August 2013, when DIA's intelligence assessments buttressed General Martin Dempsey's intervention, as Chairman of the Joint Chiefs of Staff, to force President Obama to cancel orders to launch a massive bombing campaign against the Syrian government and armed forces. Flynn and DIA argued, forcefully, that the overthrow of Assad, which would have resulted from the U.S. military intervention, would have created a jihadist stronghold on the eastern Mediterranean coast, bordering on NATO territory.

According to DIA sources, Gen. Flynn also provided critical intelligence to Defense Secretary Chuck Hagel, prompting Hagel's early October 2014 private email to National Security Advisor Dr. Susan Rice, blasting the Obama White House's failure to devise a coherent strategy for dealing with Syria.

By the time the Hagel memo was written, Gen. Flynn, along with his top deputy, had been fired from the DIA. In Feb. 2015, Hagel himself was asked by President Obama to resign, after the Oct. 2014 communique to Rice was made public.

The ouster of Gen. Flynn, the dumping of Secretary of Defense Hagel, and the imminent retirement of Joint

Chiefs of Staff Chairman Gen. Martin Dempsey, have greatly increased the danger that President Obama will go flight-forward into war either in the Middle East, or directly against Russia and China.

It is in this context that the full import of the Flynn Al-Jazeera interview must be seen. In his contentious exchange with Al-Jazeera's Mehdi Hasan, Gen. Flynn went far beyond his indictment of President Obama for ignoring warnings about the rise of the Islamic State, the arms flow from Benghazi to Syrian rebels, and the truth about the 9/11/12 attacks. He called for a top-down overhaul of U.S. strategy, particularly in the Middle East.

Asked to comment on President Obama's accelerating drone warfare, his policy of targeted killings, including of American citizens, and the overthrow of Qaddafi, Flynn responded:

> I think he's too tactical. So, the examples that you just gave, Mehdi, those are all tactical examples. And I think drone strikes is a tactic. We need big leadership and we need big strategic vision right now. Strategic vision that, I believe, only the United States can provide, frankly, because just the scale of what the United States can offer the rest of the world—and we need big strategic visionary leadership that solves a problem in the Middle East that the rest of the world is part of. You know, the word "abandonment" has been used by multiple people from multiple countries about the United States. "We feel abandoned." That's not a good place for us to be. And those are pretty senior people from these governments.
>
> So if we're dropping drones, and we're killing this guy, and that guy, training 60 guys, those are tactical, narrow things that will never,—those are investments in conflict, in greater conflict. They are not investments in real strategic solutions, and there are strategic solutions for this region.
>
> Frankly, an entire new economy is what this region needs. They need to take this 15-year old, to 25 to 30-year old in Saudi Arabia, the largest segment of their population; in Egypt, the largest segment of their population, 15 to roughly 30 years old, mostly young men. You've got to give them something else to do. If you don't, they're going to turn on their own governments, and we can solve that problem.

> So that is the conversation that we have to have with them, and we have to help them do that. And in the meantime, what we have is this continued investment in conflict. The more weapons we give, the more bombs we drop, that just fuels the conflict. Some of that has to be done, but I'm looking for other solutions. I'm looking for the other side of this argument, and we're not having it; we're not having it as the United States.

Earlier in the interview, in response to a question about Israel's nuclear arsenal and the prospects for regional total nuclear disarmament, while Russia is selling nuclear power plants to several countries in the region, Flynn noted:

> It now equals nuclear development of some type in the Middle East, and now what we want,—so what we're going to see,—what I hope for is that we have nuclear (energy) development, because it also helps for projects like desalinization, getting water. Nuclear would be great if that was nuclear energy.

Asked if he would like to see Israel give up its 200 nuclear weapons, Flynn responded:

> I would love to see it, but it's not practical because, actually, nuclear energy is very clean, and it actually is so cost effective, much more cost effective for producing water from desalinization.

Flynn emphasized that the expansion of nuclear energy, while assuring non-proliferation of nuclear weapons "has to be done in a very international, inspectable way."

General Flynn's call for a new strategic vision must start with a clean-out of those individuals responsible for the "conflict only" policies of the past two presidencies of Bush and Obama. In particular, the urgently needed starting point is a top-down house-cleaning, starting with President Obama himself. The evidence presented in the DIA documents and in Gen. Flynn's recent interview, is the crucial starting point for just such a top-down overhaul. If Hillary Clinton takes advantage of Gen. Flynn's courageous and outspoken intervention, she can finish the job and assure that the United States does not trigger a global war that leads to thermonuclear extinction. Those are the real stakes.

ELN Study Warns: NATO-Russia Maneuvers Make Nuclear War More Likely

by Helga Zepp-LaRouche

Helga Zepp-LaRouche is chairwoman of Germany's Civil Rights Solidarity Movement political party (BüSo).

Aug. 15—The European Leadership Network (ELN), a think tank composed of former European and Russian defense ministers and other high-level experts, published a study August 12, warning that the ongoing military maneuvers by NATO and Russia make the possibility of a war in Europe more likely. "Russia is preparing for a conflict with NATO, and NATO is preparing for a possible confrontation with Russia," according to the report. The only thing wrong with this study is the assumption that such a war would remain confined to Europe. It is in the nature of things that such a war would instantly become a global nuclear war, and would lead to the obliteration of the human species.

A NATO spokeswoman, Carmen Romero, immediately issued a furious protest on the NATO website, saying that the NATO maneuvers by no means increase the danger of war; that all the exercises are proportional, defensive, and completely within the bounds of international obligations. Sputnik News in turn commented on this interpretation, saying that by reacting that way, NATO was showing precisely the logic that the ELN paper warned would aggravate the crisis. Wolfgang Ischinger, head of the Munich Security Conference, and an ELN Board Member, in an interview with the magazine *Das Parlament*, described the renewed arms race and diplomatic freeze between NATO and Russia as alarming. New military guidelines must be agreed upon immediately, he said, to ensure that accidents in the air, which could happen at any moment, do not lead to an "uncontrollable situation."

It is a good thing that at least people like

European Leadership Network

These two schematic maps of recent Russian and NATO maneuvers are included in the August 12 report of the European Leadership Network on the increasing probability of war.

Ischinger and former defense ministers such as Volker Rühe (Germany) and Malcolm Rifkind (U.K.), who undoubtedly are part of the Establishment, are issuing these warnings, even if they fall short of what is required. It is also useful that, precisely on the occasion of the 70th anniversary of the nuclear bombing of Hiroshima and Nagasaki, many leading figures, from Pope Francis to Japanese Prime Minister Shinzo Abe and British Labour Party politician Jeremy Corbyn, have called for banning nuclear weapons.

But it's not weapons that prepare the way for the war. It's the people who have the power to push the button, and under whose command, maneuvers such as the current ones are being carried out.

The Immediate Danger

In addition to the large number of NATO maneuvers since the Spring, "Trident Juncture 2015," the largest NATO exercise in 25 years, will take place from Sept. 28 to Nov. 6, and will include simulating the use of nuclear weapons against Russia. But it would be a total misjudgment of the seriousness of the situation to be lulled into a sense of security until that time.

In fact, there is the imminent threat that the Ukrainian Nazi organization Right Sector, which helped bring President Petro Poroshenko to power, is doing everything to sabotage the Minsk peace process. In addition to an escalation of attacks against Donetsk, with 60-80 bombardments per day by the Ukrainian Army, Kiev on August 3-4, for the umpteenth time, rejected negotiations with the subgroups of the Minsk Contact Group. These negotiations were intended to lead to the withdrawal of weapons of up to 100 mm-caliber from the front line. Denis Pushilin, representative of the People's Republic of Donetsk in the Minsk Group, told TASS: "Kiev is probably also aware that a failure of the Minsk process means war, not only in the Donbas, but it probably means a big war."

Remember that the Ukraine crisis was triggered by the EU's imperialist intention to bring that country, by means of the EU Association Agreements, into the NATO sphere of influence. The Maidan destabilization last year by the Right Sector and other Nazi groups, including the coup against the legitimately elected government of President Yanukovych, however, is fully the responsibility of U.S. Assistant Secretary of State for European and Eurasian Affairs Victoria Nuland, who made a name for herself with her "F—ck the EU" and installed her "Yats" [Arseniy Yatsenyuk] as prime minister.

Nuland, who belongs to a non-partisan war party in the United States,—along with UN Ambassador Samantha Power, National Security Advisor Susan Rice, Nuland's neocon husband Robert Kagan, Anne Applebaum, Fred Hiatt, and Anders Aslund,—represents the full continuity of the Bush-Cheney Administration into the Obama Administration. (She was principal deputy foreign policy adviser to Dick Cheney.) This grouping personifies the long-term strategy of the past 25 years of Anglo-American neocon politics: the expansion of NATO right up to the borders of Russia; the construction of a missile defense system to provide a first-strike capacity; the color revolutions and the sanctions against Russia with the goal of regime change; and the implementation of the "Yugoslavia model"—i.e., the territorial breakup of Russia.

Christian Neumann, a member of the Darmstadt Signal, an organization of anti-militarist Bundeswehr officers, has underlined the importance of Law 2953, which Kiev adopted on June 4. It allows the stationing of foreign troops in Ukraine, including the short-term deployment of nuclear weapons and other weapons of mass destruction. Under this option the escalation of a war into a nuclear war would be imminent.

The People Must Rise Up

The overall global situation presents an incredible picture: Nuland is in charge of the escalation in Ukraine, a situation that has the potential to trigger a nuclear war between NATO and Russia. Meanwhile, the revelations of former head of the U.S. Defense Intelligence Agency Gen. Michael Flynn—that Obama consciously decided to build up the Islamic State (ISIS), knowing full well that ISIS was planning an Islamist Caliphate in Syria and Iraq—are being reported in countless media.

The change in the rules of engagement for the U.S. Air Force in Syria, without the consent of the Congress, could also be the spark for a major Middle East war, which could lead to world war. The escalation in the South China Sea is also not China's fault, but traces back to the geopolitical manipulation at the Paris Conference of 1919, and is the result of the Obama Administration's "Asia pivot" strategy.

This is the context for the warnings of the ELN think tank. In other words, we are seeing an escalation, over these days and weeks, that will result in the nuclear annihilation of mankind, if it is not stopped.

As I said, it is not weapons that cause wars, but the Commanders in Chief who decide to use them. One would think that no one would disagree that playing

with the risk of a global thermonuclear war is the sign of a deranged moral and intellectual consciousness. In the United States, Lyndon LaRouche is therefore calling for the immediate removal of Obama on the basis of the 25th Amendment to the Constitution. This amendment was introduced in Congress in 1965 by Sen. Birch Bayh and Rep. Emanuel Celler, to close a legal loophole in connection with the presidential succession. This amendment played the decisive role in the resignation of President Nixon.

For us in Germany, the question remains what the government of Chancellor Merkel is doing to prevent the annihilation of Germany,—because that's what would happen in the event of a nuclear conflict between NATO and Russia. But,—and this is not at all meant cynically,—it would be all the same for us whether the war were limited to Europe, as some intend, or whether there were a global war. In either case, Germany would be wiped out.

Since we can be sure that the government has at least the same information as the ELN group, the question remains why Merkel, Vice Chancellor Sigmar Gabriel, and Defense Minister Ursula von der Leyen are keeping quiet about this existential threat. It was bad enough that the Federal Government trampled on all the rights of the population in the scandal over NSA spying in Germany. It is intolerable for Germany to support a policy of confrontation against Russia and China, putting the existence of our own country at risk.

The Federal Government is hereby called upon to withdraw immediately from the treaty on the stationing of foreign troops in Germany, and thus, the storage of tactical nuclear weapons in Germany. Germany must immediately lift the sanctions against Russia and enter into a constructive dialogue with Putin about all relevant issues.

All citizens are hereby called upon to bring onto the streets a broad movement for peace, and to force this government to either stand up for the continued existence of Germany, or to resign. The German population is currently divided into two groups: those who have understood that the hour has struck, and those who believe that they will profit from the current system of globalization. The latter prefer to live in a virtual cloud-cuckoo-land, and are ready to literally go there over dead bodies.

The question is: Are there enough people in the first category who will now stand up and make sure that Germany will continue to exist?

This article was translated from German.

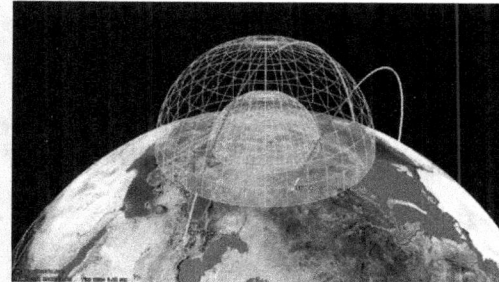

Every Day Counts In Today's Showdown To Save Civilization

That's why you need *EIR*'s **Daily Alert Service**, a strategic overview compiled with the input of Lyndon LaRouche, and delivered to your email 5 days a week.

For example: On July 27 Lyndon LaRouche identified this August as a period of maximum danger that President Barack Obama will launch provocations against Russia that could lead to the thermonuclear extinction of mankind.

EIR's July 28 Alert featured LaRouche's evaluation, along with critical intelligence on the Russian strategic doctrine. Throughout the rest of the week, the Alert has pointed to the way Hillary Clinton's exposure of Obama could interrupt Obama's war drive—as well as updates on the worsening threat.

This is intelligence you need to act on, if we are going to survive as a nation and a species. Can you really afford to be without it?

The Quality of Leadership Which Can Prevent an Imminent Thermonuclear War

Here is a transcript of excerpts from Lyndon LaRouche's Dialogue with the Manhattan Project on Saturday, August 15, 2015.

Dennis Speed: I'm Dennis Speed and on the behalf of the LaRouche Political Action Committee, I want to welcome everybody here today, for our ongoing Manhattan dialogue with Lyndon LaRouche. On Aug. 15th, 1971, Lyndon LaRouche became famous and infamous in the United States for his extraordinary apparent forecast of the collapse of the Bretton Woods System. Today, Lyndon LaRouche is also highly controversial for the fact that he is making the point that the President of the United States Barack Obama must be immediately removed from office in order to prevent the danger of an immediate outbreak of thermonuclear war.

So for a period of over 44 years, right there, this man has been in the forefront of making it clear to the world that truth speaks to power, and truth can win. So, on behalf of everybody here, I want to welcome Lyn for our dialogue, today, and I'd like us to start our questions right away. The mike is open and the first questioner should come to the microphone.

Q: Lyn, I'm A—. This week, 70 years ago, I was an aircraft mechanic, on a ship on my way to Okinawa to do conventional bombing of Japan, when we were told that we were going to Tinian instead, that the Japanese had surrendered.

There on Tinian, I saw the two B-29s that dropped the atom bombs on Hiroshima and Nagasaki; they had the names the *Enola Gay* and the *Great Artiste*. I was in awe of seeing them, and I memorized those names.

But what did you think of that time? And what do you think now, based on your historical work since then?

Lyndon LaRouche: Well, I think that my views at that time were pretty much the same as today. Because

---

> We're dealing now with a President, who, we would say in the vernacular, is no damned good; worse than no damned good. He right now, this President, is moving to launch a thermonuclear war attack, that kind of a warfare attack, which if it occurred, would begin by a launch of thermonuclear weapons against Russia. Immediately after that, there would be a reply from Russia. So the question is, do we eliminate Obama from the authority of the United States? Or do we create a situation in which most of the human species would be wiped out, exterminated? That's the issue right now.

---

the actual dropping of the bombs, as Douglas MacArthur himself emphasized, was totally unnecessary, and was against the President of the United States committing a crime against humanity, and he was aware of this thing. And that's often been the case: that political ambitions of certain kinds of people cause unnecessary danger, and damage, to humanity.

Remove Obama

What actually happened, Japan never really recovered from the fact that it, totally defeated, helpless, and totally defeated, in two locations of bombing,—has never yet recovered from that effect. Something which was totally unnecessary, unjustified in any way! Japan was a totally defeated nation, a nation which had accepted its defeat and was preparing to find a new way to adapt itself under these conditions. And what happened is, the United States government, the President of the United States, committed a crime against humanity, a *bitter* crime, a *massive* crime, in two locations; and the world has not yet recovered, from the effect on Japan of that bombing, of those two locations. And that's what you have to think about.

We're dealing now with a President, who, we would say in the vernacular, is no damned good; worse than no damned good. He, right now, this President, is moving to launch a thermonuclear war attack, that kind of a warfare attack, which, if it occurred, would begin by a launch of thermonuclear weapons against Russia. Immediately after that, there would be a reply from Russia.

In other words, the war would start by British interests such as Obama. Obama would launch the war. And then the world would fight the war. And the only response of any significance, would be Russia's reaction to the attack from the United States by Obama! So the question is, do we eliminate Obama from the authority of the United States? Or do we create a situation in which most of the human species would be wiped out, exterminated? That's the issue right now.

Q: Thank you. I'm J——, I'm a UN representative with an NGO serving child welfare victims of warfare. And I am here as a guest of François Bonneau, whose photography of the Nagasaki-Hiroshima victims is in the back, and is a voice of the legacy of any wars that leave survivors. And right now in the world, over 210 million homeless orphans exist, without education, care, water, hygiene, health care—they have *nothing*. They live outside the grid of society, and they are survivors of the hatred of war and the industry that war builds.

So today, is India's national Independence Day; I'm an honored guest of Meera Gandhi [CEO of the Giving Back Foundation] who is bringing me to meet Ambassador Mulay, and I didn't know if you had any message you'd like me to relay to him.

Man is Not an Animal

But we're doing an event at the UN on Oct. 14th to address this issue of homeless orphans, victims of warfare, and it'll be at the Scandinavia House; it's an all-day conference.

And I'd appreciate anything that you could give me to mention to the Ambassador today, or anything that you would like said.

We are all going to die, but that's not in itself a bad thing. The point is, what comes out of the life that has passed? Where's the progress for the life which has passed? Where's the fruit of the life which had passed? Where's the future beyond the life that has passed? These are the questions which, we can always remember,—for example you go to the case of the Renaissance, the Great Renaissance, and you find exactly that.

LaRouche: Well, the obvious thing is that we are operating on the basis of an actually wrong opinion of the responsibility we have to perform. Our job is to recognize that mankind, as a species, is not an animal. That mankind has a mission which no animal has, because no animal has the capability of creating a higher order of development, of a species, i.e. the human species. No other type of living being can have that operation.

In other words, our purpose as human beings in life, is—we are all going to die, in due course, shall we say. It happens eventually. The question is: What do we pass, from a presently living population to its successors, and how do we improve upon what has been achieved by man after that point. And that's what the issue is. Because we're all going to die, so therefore what is the meaning of human life? It's the meaning of human life as expressed, in the fruit of advances and improvement of conditions of human life, which enables mankind to achieve goals, which otherwise mankind could not achieve. And therefore, the inspiration, and education of our citizens, our people, in achieving higher levels of insight into the universal, itself, as mankind can do it, and that's what the issue is.

So therefore, whenever we see people who should not be abused, we must serve that principle, and operate on the basis of creating an atmosphere in society in general, which is suited to mankind's progress to a higher organization of life, a higher level of achievement of humanity. And therefore, all the pains and aches and defeats, must be dissolved into a recognition that mankind must progress to a higher level of achievement than at any time before. And that's the mission. That's the thing, that is love of mankind. Love *of* mankind is the devotion to this mission.

Q: Well, we hope to achieve that with this event, to build a great respect and love for our children, whose future we have a debt to secure, as a society, as government, as business. So that's very beautiful. Thank you.

We're All Going to Die, But...

Q: Good afternoon, Lyn, it's B— from New Jersey. Given the anniversary today of Aug. 15th, and your forecast of the change from the Bretton Woods system, at that time, I had just previous to that date, Aug. 15th, 1971, served my last year in the service, and had returned from overseas. So I think it would be important for you to reflect for people, both the basis upon which you made the forecast, and also looking at the decades since that event, what're we looking at, and what are we looking at now?

LaRouche: Take the case of great people, great scientists; what is their contribution? The great scientist is a person who foresees the necessity of a change in mankind's behavior, which increases the power of mankind to take charge over the Solar System essentially, right now. And it's the development of those creative capabilities, where people make discoveries which had never been known until those discoveries had been induced. And that is the real, underlying principle on which the importance of humanity, the human species depends.

We are all going to die, but that's not in itself a bad thing. The point is, what comes out of the life that has passed? Where's the progress for the life which has passed? Where's the fruit of the life which had passed? Where's the future beyond the life that has passed? These are the questions which, we can always remember,—for example, you go to the case of the Renaissance, the Great Renaissance, and you find exactly that.

The Renaissance was crushed, in a certain period at the beginning of the [Sixteenth] Century. But then, we

have the achievements at a higher level. So after the Great Renaissance was a force that was crushed, yet, it came back at a higher level, and that is the thing which should make us feel good. If we can achieve something that mankind has heretofore not been able to achieve, and we have gone through the strains and so forth that go with achieving that, that is a satisfactory result, for us, on the birth of our own death: the fact that our life

---

The Renaissance was crushed, in a certain period at the beginning of the [Sixteenth] Century. But then, we have the achievements at a higher level. So after the Great Renaissance was a force that was crushed, yet, it came back in a higher level, and that is the thing which should make us feel good. If we can achieve something that mankind has heretofore not been able to achieve, and we have gone through the strains and so forth that go with achieving that, that is a satisfactory result for us, on the birth of our own death, the fact that our life has meant something for the future of mankind, to lead mankind to a condition which is beyond, and superior, to what we've experienced beforehand.

---

has meant something for the future of mankind, to lead mankind to a condition which is beyond, and superior, to what we've experienced beforehand.

As long as we can have that, if we can die with the idea that we are dying on the birth of a higher level of achievement, than we had achieved in our own lives. And that is the thing that makes the dying man content.

Fighting for Glass-Steagall

Q: Hello, I'm J— from New York, and I have with me C—, also from Brooklyn, New York, and I have a short—I hope it's as short as possible—report to give, because C— and I, and one of our full-time organizers went to something called "Congress on Your Corner" this morning. "Congress on Your Corner" is a brainchild of Hakeem Jeffries, my Congressperson. So, since I'm a constituent of Congressman Jeffries, I have come into contact with him several times. I first came into contact with him in his office, when he first started as Congressperson, and since that time I have seen him in Washington, D.C.; I've seen him at his office, and various locations all around Brooklyn.

So, today he had a "Congress on Your Corner", and

I invited C—, a new member, to come, and we would confront him on the issues which we are talking about now. And this is my brief report.

I said to him: "Right now, this President is using NATO and other illegal and immoral military operations to provoke Russia, and launch World War III." He said to me, "You're wrong. Russia is the problem." And I said, "No, our President is the problem, and those who would allow him to do this, are the problem." and he said, "Well, I'm not at liberty to talk about this right now; maybe we can talk about this later," and I said, "Oh, great. I will come to your office with a group of people this week! Just let me know when you'll be there," and he shoved me off to one of his aides, and said, "Give her my card, and you call the office, and we'll talk about this."

I said, "Okay, but I still have something else to talk about: We're going to talk about Glass-Steagall! You have not signed off on Glass-Steagall and I have confronted you, and asked you to do this several times."

He goes, "Oh yes. Uh, let me see what you have…" So, I showed him my "visual," [displays leaflet] and then he said, "Oh, there has been something introduced into the Senate."

And I said, "Yes, I have that right here!" So, I showed him that, and then, he started to sweat a little bit—I mean, it was hot (chuckles), but still.…

And he said, "Oh yes, Elizabeth Warren," and he started reading it: "Oh yes, yes! Oh, well, you know, I'm taking this into consideration."

And I said, "But you've been taking this into consideration for three years already!"

He goes, "Yes, I understand that, but you know the bill is different; when they introduce another bill, it's a little different, it's worded a little different; I have to look it over, there's different committees."

And I said, "You know what? I think the bill basically is the same. The policy that Glass-Steagall represents, the constitutional principle that Glass-Steagall represents, is the same."

So, he said to me, "You know, I admire your persistence. [laughter] Miss W—" and this is the good part, "Miss W—, I will look into this, and we will talk."

"Miss W—!" OK! [laughter]

So!, That is where I got with Mr. Hakeem. Now, he wasn't as slippery as he usually is, so we did—at least

creative commons

Marcy Kaptur (D-Ohio) has led the fight to restore Glass-Steagall in the House of Representatives for several years. Her bill, HR 381, now has 66 sponsors. Here, she speaks at the House Committee on Education and the Workforce in March 2012.

we'll get somewhere. and that's my report.

LaRouche: [laughter] Very good! [applause]

What John Kennedy Did

Q: Good afternoon, Mr. LaRouche. I'm P— from Connecticut. In 1961, I was stationed in West Germany, when the Berlin Wall went up. And, then in 1962, when the Cuban crisis escalated, the 13 days of October, I was with the 3rd Missile Battalion, 21st Artillery, three kilometers from the Czech border, with our "Honest John" missiles, armed and ready. They were thermonuclear warheads.

I was 18 years old, and I was scared to death of the outcome. We, in our training, had seen films of the destruction of atomic weapons. And working with them, we had a good knowledge of what the destruction was: And that's annihilation.

My question is: What is the difference between the Cuban Crisis, and the crisis we have today?

LaRouche: That's a very clear thing, and easy for me to respond to. What we had was a threat of thermonuclear war between Russia and the United States. We had a President at that time, who organized with Russia to avoid a thermonuclear war; this happened in the so-called Cuba Crisis. What happened with that, is the President who had done that job of negotiating the avoidance of a thermonuclear war, the most serious thermonuclear war that the United States had ever experienced—was averted by the President of the United States, in collaboration with the Soviet Union, representatives of the Soviet Union. That avoided it!

Obama and Evil Force

Soon, apparently some people in the United States were not happy about the fact that we had not gone to a thermonuclear war, which had been prevented by the President of the United States. And not so mysteriously then, the President of the United States was himself assassinated by services which were not, shall we say, to our liking.

And today, we're still going through the same kind of thing: Right now, we have Obama. And Obama is now deployed by various circles, including British circles and other circles, to conduct warfare which, if taken forward, would mean the virtual extinction of the human species. That's what the problem is right now.

The problem is political, because what has happened is, a careful culling and adjustment of governmental positions, in order to "encourage" assassinations of that type, rather than preventing them. That's what it's all about.

So we are actually involved in saying: Obama is now the evil force. Obama is a person who should be thrown out of office immediately, for the sake of all humanity. He's a mass murderer. And he's setting up this side, for a war to be launched, probably this month or into early next month. When the war that Obama intends to cause, will bring humanity to the threshold of extermination, in fact.

The situation is such that Russia will not launch the war. Obama will launch the war! Russia will not react, unless Obama has moved to launch thermonuclear war. And that's the situation right now.

So, anybody who is defending Obama's policy is, wittingly or not, condemning mankind to the threat of extermination. That's the fight. That's the *fact* of the matter. And, what we can do to prevent Obama from proceeding on his intention, is the most noble thing that any citizen of the United States can undertake.

Q: Hello, Mr. LaRouche, my name is J—; I'm from

Xinhua/Wu Dengfeng

Readiness to respond: Here China and Russia carry out one of their recent series of naval maneuvers, this time in the Yellow Sea in April 2012.

the Bronx. I have a question about China. Not too long ago, the IMF ... [technical interruption]. Basically, those very circles that you're talking about that control Obama, are they trying secretly, to instigate the war, basically with that explosion that happened in China not too long ago, just the day after they devalued their currency?

And also, is there any significance in what's going on in Cuba right now, where they just re-opened the U.S. Embassy? So, both of those things,—I just want to know your opinion about.

The Commitment to Depopulation

LaRouche: I think the Cuba situation presently more or less speaks for itself. There are various ways in which you could interpret what might have been the preferred way of dealing with this question of resolving a reconciliation between the United States and Cuba; and the very fact of that reconciliation is useful. But with the only qualification is, can Cuba trust the Obama Administration? That is the question there. No, but that is not the problem.

The problem is, there is a process, a commitment to launch a change in behavior, to reduce the population of the planet, under British direction and under the current Pope himself; to reduce the population of the people on Earth, to reduce it to a small part, to a great reduction of the entire population of the planet.

We see it all throughout our own area: For example,

in California, the governor in California is proposing a genocide policy to reduce the population of California. A massive reduction of the population of California, done by the governor of California right now.

And other things like that are going on. The green policy, the so-called green policy, is a policy of intentional genocide, against the majority of the population, the U.S. population and the world's population.

So these are things one has to be aware of, and once aware of these things and understanding what the nature of them is, we've got to *stop* that kind of process. We've got to shut down the governor of California, who is *for* genocide against mankind; and it's unforgivable, it is intolerable.

And those are the kinds of conditions, which we have to face, and most citizens of the United States, as citizens, are worried about this kind of situation, but they lack an understanding of an approach to deal with the threat. What I am responsible to do, on my part, is to try to make clear the nature of the threat, and to get people like the current governor of California out of office, because he is a threat to all humanity, whether he intends it or not.

The Queen Is Impotent

Q: My name is S— from New York City, and I have one question which I will ask in a moment, but three comments—that you can choose to comment on or not! [laughter]

It's very seldom I get to ask a person of your stature questions like this. The first comment is—which is kind of a question, really—where are the back-channels, the channels that we had during the Cuban missile crisis? You don't have to answer that right now. Where are the back channels? You're probably going to say there are none.

The other thing is, why do we see a mobilization of United Nations' vehicles across the U.S.A.?

And the other thing is, it seems as if the U.S. is prepping for mass casualties. Now here's the question—just keep those things in the back of your mind, the other things. The question is, why do we see in the City of London, I guess you could say, conflicting activities in that the City of London, the British Empire, tells us *not* to join the BRICS alliance and *not* to join the Asia bank [AIIB], yet *they* join the Asia bank? Which is the right thing to do, as a charter member, yet we don't. So is

Climate Scientist: Encyclical Laudato Si' mirrors scientific findings

The British Monarchy's plans for global depopulation were strongly advanced with the Vatican's bringing in depopulator John Schellnhuber into preparations for the Pope's Laudato Si' *encyclical. Here, Schellnhuber on the dais when the encyclical was presented in Rome June 18, 2015.*

there like some in-fighting in the City of London, that is telling us *not* to do something good, but yet they're doing the right thing? Are they trying to infiltrate the Asia bank? Or are they doing it because they know it's the right thing to do?

LaRouche: Well, there are certain complexities in answering that question, because first of all, what happened is, the British Monarchy, the Queen and so forth, is incompetent. That is, they've reached a stage of life where the skull-part doesn't work too well. They are paraded around in dress, in popular dress, but their thinking processes are not really functional.

Now this has a cause to it and an implication to it. That you have now a revolt from the Labour Party, which is actually moving against the monarchy, and what the monarchy represents. And this is because the failure of the mental life of the British monarchy, the British Empire forces, these forces are degenerate. And what has happened,—this creates an opening, where you now have a part of the Labour Party in London, which is moving in a contrary direction, which is quite useful in itself. It's the Labour Party, and it's well-organized, fairly well. And the Queen and so forth and her retinue are actually totally impotent.

A Big Question Mark

Now there are forces which are trying to use them, use these institutions, but the smell is out in London. And the British have been put through this thing so many times, they tend to catch on to what is being done to them. And when somebody gets an organization going inside the British system, or the United Kingdom system, including Scotland and so forth, when this happens, there tends to be a revolt. They say, "Do we have to put up with this any more? Do we have to put up with this any more?" And I find that a very healthy symptom, in terms of what the leadership is of the Labour Party in Britain now. I think it's an optimistic turn.

But the other side is, what's the alternative? And the alternative is, to let them hope that they win in Britain in the coming election which is now coming up, in order to save us from the dangers which otherwise would come from that quarter. So this has good sides to it, the fact that there's a Labour Party movement which is actually makes a lot of sense. Whereas the leading forces otherwise, are bad forces and will lead to destruction.

So I think this is something on which there is a big question mark of how things are going to turn out, but I think we can be more optimistic, or less un-optimistic than we have heretofore.

Q: [followup] What do the people in the City of London think about the whole Wall Street situation?

LaRouche: Wall Street has to be buried. We have to get rid of Wall Street. Cut it out, Glass-Steagall— straight Glass-Steagall, the way that Franklin Roosevelt defined it. Get right back to that, straight.

Q: [followup] Thank you very much. Don't forget about the other three things I mentioned, okay? The UN vehicles, the back-channels, and why are we prepping for mass casualties?

LaRouche: Well look, we all are involved in back-channels; we're all doing that, who are active.

Q: I am K— from the Bronx. One of your people told me that one of the candidates in London is for Glass-Steagall.

LaRouche: Yes.

Q: [followup] I just thought I'd toss that in.

On your Thursday night program, there was a discussion about how the Nazis got in to Ukraine, along that line. I have read that Allen Dulles, who was in the Truman Administration, as I understand, had protected the Nazis in Ukraine from being put on trial, so as to save them for another day. And if that's true, the day has certainly come.

Hillary's Mistake

LaRouche: Well that's true. That *is* the fact. Allen Dulles *was* exactly that kind of person. The two brothers. And the Dulles brothers were two of the most evil people in the recent history of the United States.

Q: [followup] And there's been a lot of evil people.

LaRouche: Oh yes! We are abundantly supplied with evil people. The question is, how do we get them in the proper cages, where they can do no more harm?

Q: [followup] What I wanted to mention to you is about Hillary Clinton. She has stated that she has not used her personal computer for Secretary of State emails, and that she's innocent. Well, the FBI is investigating her, and we are all very excited about the fact that there are Dick Tracys in the FBI looking at her emails. What I understand, is, that the head of the Department of Justice was selected or recommended by Al Sharpton, and Hillary Clinton is friends with Al Sharpton and the head of the DOJ. And it is anticipated that they are going to give her a clean bill of health.

LaRouche: I wouldn't buy into that. I don't think that it's that simple. I think that Hillary, who has made terrible mistakes, became disoriented because she capitulated to Obama. She had a choice not to support Obama, and she didn't realize what an evil, Satanic figure this guy is, and already was. And therefore she got trapped. And what she did—she tried to tell the truth on the issue at one point. But he came down on her like a hammer, and she capitulated. So she did not have the guts to face up to what he represents. But you have to say, this guy is actually—Obama is really a satanic figure. We don't know how Satanist he is, but we know his behavior is Satanic.

And the problem is that we have this Satanic character, who's now almost gone through two terms of service, but we had also before then, the Bush family, Bush administration was just as evil or more evil, than what is in. So the problem is, we have not had honest candidates elected to the Presidency in [fifteen] years. And the effect shows.

Preventing Nuclear War

Now we have a group of people of Congress, in the institutions of the Congress, and institutions of the government, who do want to prevent this. Those people, who are of the military and so forth, or other categories of this type, are determined to prevent what Obama's doing; Obama and his backers have chopped off the au-

CC/U.S. State Dept.

Sen. Tim Kaine, one of the few Congressional voices speaking out against Obama's war drive in Southwest Asia. Here he speaks in 2014.

thority of leading figures who had been the safeguards of our civilization, in those years.

Right now, during this period, from the Spring into the present time, there has been a process of destroying the safeguards which existed, actually inside the Obama Administration. But now Obama has moved to strip all the authorities which had been curbs of his travesties, and we're coming up to the edge, where he is in a position, probably this month or next month, to launch a thermonuclear war on a global basis.

Because what's planned is, that he would launch a thermonuclear war against Russia and other locations. That's what the situation is. If that were to happen, then you would have, probably an extermination of much of the human species, if not all of it. And what we're trying to do now, is prevent that thing from happening in that way. And the chances of defeating this kind of evil, are getting thinner and thinner.

And I'm very much involved in this stuff, this particular issue. I know that there're people in government who are trying to prevent this; they're important people, they have certain powers; we have members of Congress who are in a position to block this process, but we're having very soft treatment of this problem, from my standpoint.

We are in a fight, from our state and through other forces on other parts of the planet, we're in a struggle to prevent Obama from launching a thermonuclear war, whose result would be the virtual extermination of most of the human species.

Q: There's a chance of a military coup?

LaRouche: Well, people know it! There's no lack of people who know this information, who know this threat. But the question is, who has the guts to stand up against Obama? That's what the issue is. He's evil, there's no question of that. The question, who's going to get rid of him. Put him in a bucket someplace. [Speed laughs]

It Can Be Stopped

Q: Hi, Mr. LaRouche.

LaRouche: Hi. I know you. I remember you.

Q: This is E— from the Bronx. My question is, the world is in such a threat of a nuclear war, now, God forbid—I would just like to ask, can music and art do anything to alleviate that situation, to make it so that that should not happen? That's my question, really.

LaRouche: OK, yeah, well, I'm working at that, and I'm optimistic about the possibility of winning. But I don't have any certainty of a success. I will do everything that I can, within my capabilities, and I've had a lot of experience with this sort of thing; you know, at my age and the activities I've lived through, I've been pretty much experienced in a very significant way, with various parts of the planet. It's been my career in life. And therefore, I do know things that can work, and I often advise people in important circles to what my opinions are, as to what can be done to stop these things.

But in my capacity speaking here, I have to present, actually the fuller possibilities of what can happen. My involvement is to inform people, usefully, in things that might work, which is what I do anyway. But I do not intend to have doom coming down on the United States, or the world as a whole; I just don't intend to sit back and say that's going to happen. I will say, that is what is threatened, and therefore let us take heed, and let us take the actions which can be effective; let's find out what we can do to stop this nonsense. And I, of course, have an advantage because of my experience; that's really all I have is my experience and the reflections of my experience.

But I do know that it's possible to defeat this process. The question is, are we going to mobilize the forces, to do it? I'm not a pessimist. [applause]

EIRNS/Stuart Lewis

The world was deprived of excellent global leadership when Indian Prime Minister Indira Gandhi was assassinated in 1984. Here she speaks at the National Press Club in Washington on July 30, 1982.

With Indira Gandhi and Ronald Reagan

Q: Hi Lyn, this is A—, and I too am from the Bronx.

Earlier in this webcast it was brought up about the celebrations that the people of India are putting on today, because of their defeat and rejection of, I don't know how many hundreds of years of colonialism. And in India, you're very familiar with it, you had an ongoing, working relationship with Indira Gandhi,—they are, of course, making headway in the BRICS; we see some scientific progress.

What I'd like to know from you, is what other changes are required in that nation, so that they can take the real Promethean leadership, and join China and end up working at the same level that China is operating on now?

LaRouche: I was very close to Indira Gandhi, personally. We met a number of times, and I was committed to her cause and so forth, and I was committed to her family, as such, as a leadership as such, as a leadership at that time. And she and I would be on the phones and so forth, we would discuss things of that nature from time to time, on projects she would have, and I would have projects of that nature.

And what happened, of course, the British Empire assassinated her. And the assassination of Indira Gandhi

was very important. For example, just to get an appreciation of the situation: Indira was studying as a student in Switzerland. And while she was in that process of maturing to this kind of position, she was very close to Charles de Gaulle, President Charles de Gaulle. And he admired her greatly for her intellect, in the meeting that he had held for her in the Switzerland area. And she was great.

But the problem is, as is often the case in history, that a great woman, like her, when assassinated, creates a vacuum in the continuity of the process of a great nation, India in this case. And what happened was, she became irreplaceable in fact.

Now, this was a period when I was working with the President of the United States, and I was acting as a mediating force between Indira and our President [Reagan] at the time—and then she's knocked out. So a very important link between Indira Gandhi and the President of the United States, was broken. And we all suffered. And of course, he was shot by an associate of the Bush family, and that was a weakness.

So you have an overlap of cases of people who were great leaders, and he was a great leader before he got shot. I worked for him; I was part of his staff, in his intelligence staff. I organized a whole organization for him on that basis. But then he was shot. He survived, but he was crippled to a significant degree, and other forces took over much of his authority, during the rest of his term as President.

Leadership is Decisive

And that happens. These kinds of things happen. And forces that are destructive will go and target leading persons in society; in other words, you cannot just go out and recruit somebody to be something as a leader. It does not work in history. History depends upon leaders who are competent and reliable. That's how history works. Democracy *per se* is bunk when it comes to that issue. Democracy is as sufficient as the leadership we can provide. That's the general case in history.

And that's the case right now: The role of leadership, in nations, is among the most decisive, and therefore most important, considerations in all politics, especially all national politics and international politics. If you don't have an exceptional person, or persons, in leadership, in government, you probably are going to have the kind of failure we've had under Bush, and now under Obama. And the mistakes we made were having Bush, and having Obama.

Q: Good afternoon, Mr. LaRouche. I am V— of Brooklyn. Mr. LaRouche, you and your team are developing a new paradigm of creative mind of mankind, opposing the point of view on the human as being like just another animal. What would your answer be to the people who defend and spread the ideas that only actually a small percent of the population has the kind of ability of creative mind? And most of the people are actually more like an animal? And of course, countries, by their thoughts, have to be ruled by and in favor of this small percent of the population?

LaRouche: Well, the

kremlin.ru

Leadership means creating a force "to accomplish the mission of serving the nation, serving the culture, serving the future." Here, Russian President Vladimir Putin (center) and Chinese President Xi Jinping (right) at the May 8, 2015 military parade in Moscow, marking the 70th anniversary of V-E Day.

point goes to the question of what is the standard of leadership, in society? You could take the case of Russia, for example, because Russia has a history which is an easy map to read, to show the evolution of what the fluctuations and destiny of Russia have been, over conditions, particularly under the current leader in Russia. And so, you find, when you look at that, if you look at it from the Russian standpoint, leadership is a very important question. And when Russians are smart, they're very careful, in terms of leadership, of how they operate themselves in order to create a force which will enable them to accomplish the mission of serving the nation, serving the culture, serving the future.

The Leadership We Need

And so therefore, this question is crucial. You cannot simply say, we're going to elect some guy and put a wig on his head, huh? and call him a genius. That is not a very good idea. So therefore, what you have to do, you have to cultivate, in society,—we have to cultivate people who are sometimes called geniuses. They're not always actually geniuses, but they function in a way in which, together with other people, they form the effect of the act of genius.

You'll often find in nations that there is a bunch of people, who together, represent a genius, a quality of judgment which solves a major problem for mankind.

And that's what we're up against. We have the case of like, what you're having in the neighboring area here: We have a Nazi organization running the organization which is now confronting Russia; it's a Nazi organization. It was born of the Nazis, of Hitler Nazis. It's now the ruling force in Ukraine society. This element is used by the British and others, to try to destroy Russia.

Russia has to deal with this, with a very delicate way of approaching this thing. Because Germany, which should be supporting Russia in this case,—because German interests and Russian interests are identical in terms of the economic process right now, the cooperation between the skills of Germany, in the best industries in Germany, and the skills of Russia, must be things which are adjoined.

And the problem is, if we don't have qualities of leadership which are both intelligent, and determined to take the actions which prevent disaster, disaster generally tends to happen. Most of the disasters in human history are the result of a lack of competent leadership. Or the leadership may have been there, but they were not allowed to function.

And in Russia right now, I think they're in pretty good shape in terms of Putin. I know him in a sense; I've never talked with him directly—I have talked with him indirectly a number of times—but he's quite a capable character. He's done an excellent job in what he's done. But the point is, you just think, what if he's assassinated? And I'm sure he thinks about those kinds of things some times; he knows that his assassination is a serious threat to Russia itself, and to society in general.

Producing Geniuses

We're in a real mess in terms of these things, and we have to understand what the issues are, and we have to

---

Now, people always think about the individual genius; now the individual genius in society is an important phenomenon. There's no question about that. Einstein demonstrates that very clearly. But, the point is, the individual genius can be over-exaggerated. Geniuses wherever they occur may be necessary. But what's necessary is people around the genius, so-called, who are capable of understanding what they have to do with the talent that's been dumped in their hands. And therefore, if you don't have a society that is resonant with an understanding of what society needs, for its own existence, for its own development, it's a failure.

---

use that to *flank the enemy*. We have to determine what the forces that are causing the trouble, and we try to flank it; rather than making war against it, we try to flank it. and the principle of the flank, I think, is the great mystery that has to be unravelled.

Q: Don't you think that we depend too much on leadership, on geniuses having to be in the leadership, and maybe some political system needs to give more power to the people?

LaRouche: That doesn't work. Because unless the people have among themselves—among their own population—have the ability to muster genius, genius will not be manifest, and catastrophe will probably result as a lack of that genius. Geniuses are—real geniuses—a leadership of genius, are essential to the success of society. And therefore, that's why education is so important, why scientific study is so important. You have the people who represent the elements of genius, which means the increase of the power of mankind, to create beyond what mankind has known before. And you want to produce people who have the quality of genius.

And a true genius is always a very modest person, because a true genius always recognizes the danger which they face, not only in terms of threats to them, but in terms their own failures. [applause]

Q: Hello, Mr. LaRouche, this is H— from the Bronx. So far, what we've seen from the Presidential campaign is the Republican debates, and I wonder what we could say of various of these people, or as a group, what this phenomenon is. I mean, we have Donald Trump who goes from ridiculous to obscene; we have Mr. Kasich who is sort of the new moderate or something, we're not sure what; we have Rand Paul who occasionally does do some useful things, I think; and then of course, lurking in the background is Mr. Jeb, Jeb Bush. So I don't know quite what to make of this thing, or collectively, what we can say about this phenomenon, since one of these Republicans could actually—we don't like to even say it—but could actually go further in this process. [laughter]

We Must Become a School

LaRouche: I think you've got two types of persons. You've got persons like the FBI. Now Trump is a product of the FBI organization; his family is, that's his location. And he's a thug, he's a bum, he's a liar, he's a swindler, he has all the attributes of being a successful Republican nominee. [laughter]

On the other hand, you have the problems of failure, the lack of development of insights and practices, which are necessary for mankind to overcome the threatened disasters which are lurking around us all over the place. And what we have to do, is, we have to actually become a school, which is a very good school necessarily, for organizing society as a force.

Now, people always think about the individual genius; now the individual genius in society is an important phenomenon. There's no question about that. Einstein demonstrates that very clearly. But, the point is, the individual genius can be over-exaggerated. Geniuses, wherever they occur, may be necessary. But what's necessary is people around the genius, so-called, who are capable of understanding what they have to do with the talent that's been dumped in their hands.

Therefore, if you don't have a society that is resonant with an understanding of what society *needs*, for its own existence, for its own development, it's a failure. And what happens is, when you make people stupid, you destroy their ability to exercise good judgment; they don't know what they're talking about!

They're blocked, they're ignorant! And it's very important that we develop really intelligent people in terms of society, in all levels of society. It's not one elite alone; you find the genius often turns out to be some guy who was obscure to you beforehand; and suddenly, one day he opened his mouth and said something, and you have to realize he knew something.

So the point is, you have to have the idea of a society which shares its knowledge, shares its skill, shares the developments of its skill. And that's the thing we base ourselves on. Because you know, we all die; we're all going to die sooner or later. And so therefore, we have to worry about the supply of people who are going to carry on the job, which someone who may have passed on, was going to do otherwise. So you just have to have this idea of sharing of the intention to meet the challenges which mankind requires.

Science and Religion

Q: Hi, Mr. LaRouche, my name is Y—, and I'm 19 years old. I'm from Harlem. And I'm totally onboard with everything you're saying, and I just wanted to make a comment. I hope you can resonate with it a little bit.

I think that's definitely true that Obama has been a Satanic figure, because I feel like Satan uses people for his purposes, and he is the serpent that leads the whole world astray, as it says in Revelation 12:9. And I think that people are being deceived by all this, and people are being deceived so much that they feel like they don't have the potential to change. And I think the purpose of this group, LaRouche, is just that, is to make effective change.

I also think that it's pretty evident to all that humanity will fail because we're all imperfect. And I actually want to share a Scripture with you, if you don't mind: It's in Matthew 24:6-8. It says, Jesus is talking to His disciples and He says, "You will hear of wars and rumors of wars, but see to it that you are not alarmed. Such things must happen but the end is still to come. Nation will rise against nation and kingdom against kingdom. There will be famines and earthquakes in various places. All these are the beginnings of birth pains."

So God knows everything, and I think that Jesus is the hope, and He's the only one we should depend on for our source of strength, source of leadership, because we ourselves cannot do it alone. We're imperfect. So that's just what I have to say.

LaRouche: We don't need to be that imperfect.

"You have to understand that there's a force in the universe, which is far more powerful than we ourselves can understand. We therefore try to order ourselves and our behavior, in accord with our best understanding of what that superior force is."

That we have a certain imposition of modesty of our own talents, of course, is natural. But the progress of mankind is typified by scientific progress, true scientific progress.

For example, take the case of power, physical power; take the case of Kepler's discovery of the Solar System; take the case of the discovery of the Galaxy: These are arranged in an order, where you go from mankind's ordinary abilities, you go to a higher level as Kepler represents this higher level of a principle; it goes to the idea of the Galactic principle, which is a still higher principle.

Relying on What You Don't Yet Know

So that the question about the Deity comes in, that the Deity is more than anything that we know in these categories. And yet, we are dependent upon that influence. What we think, in terms of religion, is the fact that there is a force in the universe, which is operating on us, in our setting, and if we can understand that force and respond to it, we can recognize such things as the people who discovered the Solar System; the forces who then discovered later, the higher order, the Galactic System; and beyond that, what we have yet to discover. We have inklings of this, inklings of that.

So we find that we live in a universe, which is ruled by something higher than anything that man knows presently. And yet, we're able to experience some aspects of that knowledge, and we respond to it on the basis of our recognition, that this is a valid influence, even though our own knowledge is imperfect in that.

And in the practice of life, that's what's most important. Can we, when mankind is faced with a great problem, like right now—*right now*, we're on the threat of the extermination of the human species under Obama and similar people, to wipe us off the planet *right now*, in this month or the next month! It's there!

So therefore, we rely not only on what we are able to do, we also have to rely upon things that we do not yet understand, but recognize that they are an option, which may be the solution. And therefore, we look at the idea of Deity which is a power which is greater than anything that mankind can really understand, and you try to respond to those things which you experience, as representing that power, a power of a Deity. And you try to make yourself function in coherence with that power of the Deity, which you don't really know, but you recognize the signs, you recognize the experience, you find something resonant, which fits that. And that's the best you have.

We always try to understand this better, improve our own understanding of what these processes are. Like real scientific work is of that nature. What is it, like Einstein? Einstein made a discovery of something that mankind had never known before! But Einstein is simply typical of creative forces in the human process, and you're very happy when you find someone who does that, as Einstein did. Einstein was absolutely *unique* in this respect, during the period of his life.

And so yeah, this is all true. But you don't have to give just a name to it. You have to understand that there is a force in the universe, which is far more powerful than we ourselves can understand. We therefore try to order ourselves and our behavior, in accord with our best understanding of what that superior force is. And that is what the real purpose for religious belief is: That there's a force in the universe, which is acting in a cer-

tain way, that we try to find ourselves in accord with that force. And we become personally attached to that idea of that force, and that becomes our morality. [applause]

Money Right Now is Trash

Q: Hi, Mr. LaRouche, R— from Bergen County, New Jersey. My question is, given the recent devaluation of the yuan, in your opinion could that lead to a currency war internationally, in the form of competitive devaluations, of the currency, which could lead to an implosion of the world currently system, and therefore making the issues of impeachment and Glass-Steagall just absolutely imperative this second?

LaRouche: Franklin Roosevelt's understanding of Glass-Steagall was one of the best pieces of understanding that mankind has had so far, at least in recent times.

The problem is that we are imprisoned by the idea of money; we assume that money has some intrinsic value all its own, and that if you can grab this money, hold it in your hand, kiss it! Hold it in your arms! Love it! Money!

Money right now is trash. All the wealth of Wall Street, *all* the wealth of Wall Street, is *worthless*. All its money is worthless!

How would we deal with that? It's not difficult. I know how to do that! What you have to do, is you have to produce increasing powers of labor, to advance the conditions of mankind's life. Now, that's what Franklin Roosevelt understood. And after Franklin Roosevelt was out of office, then we tended to get a lot of clowns coming in and saying, they are now going to deal with the question of *money*! We had that before Franklin Roosevelt was empowered; we had it repeatedly in terms of the history of the United States. The swindlers of the United States, the swindlers of the world, have dominated society most of the time. So people think that there's some magic out there, which enables the swindlers to win.

The problem is, the people are dumb, because they didn't take the trouble to find out what the solution is. And if we actually put Glass-Steagall into operation, *full operation*, we can solve this problem, right away.

Why Music

Q: Mr. LaRouche, good afternoon: D—. How do we start the ball rolling on Amendment 25? What can we do?

LaRouche: Okay. I'm trying to do that right now! I do it all the time. Sometimes we have some luck, and sometimes we don't. but I always intended it. I don't think we made many mistakes on this thing, but unfortunately a lot of the institutions of government have not accepted that wisdom.

Q: What has to happen in order to have him removed from office? What has to happen from the population?

LaRouche: ... difficult. I mean, the knowledge of how to organize, I have that knowledge; it's my specialty. I know exactly how to organize things like that. I've spent most of my life doing it. It works! But, you've got to shut down Wall Street and then it'll begin to work. Just get Wall Street out of Manhattan, and you might make some successes.

Speed: All right. It appears that that's all the questions for today, so I'm going to just bring up one, because it was asked of me during the music sessions. One person who was here for the first time, about 20 minutes into it, leaned over and said to me, "What exactly is this meeting for?" And then, wanted to know, "What does the music have to do, with stopping nuclear war, or politics, or *what*? Why are you doing this?"

So I thought I should ask that question, and give you a means to both respond if you wish, and also, I guess, summarize for the day.

LaRouche: OK! [laughs] Well that's feasible. No, the point is, what we do is we create forces in society which are determined by the powers of mankind's creative forces. And what you're trying to do, always, is you're trying to create something which is needed, or you think is needed, and you decide that you have to step outside ordinary practice, in order to solve the problem you've just confronted.

> That's the basis of this whole thing. Mankind has to become wiser, and it has to be a process of development. Now everything I do is based on this kind of idea of the process of development; I've spent most of my life on that. And I've found that most of the errors that occur are usually caused by ignorance. And ignorance is often caused by a refusal to investigate options which are actually creative in their effect.

> Often what happens, the practical man, so-called, is often the source of his own self-destruction. He says, "I'm practical. I'm practical." Now, in mathematics, and in science in general, that's tragic. People who are practical are intrinsically tragic, because they limit themselves to what they think is practical, whereas progress is always based on getting beyond being practical by making discoveries of principle, or discovering principles which had existed before, but you hadn't understood them.

The Practical Man is Stupid

That's the basis of this whole thing. Mankind has to become wiser, and it has to be a process of development. Now everything I do is based on this kind of idea of the process of development; I've spent most of my life on that. And I've found that most of the errors that occur are usually caused by ignorance. And ignorance is often caused by a refusal to investigate options which are actually creative in their effect.

Often what happens, the practical man, so-called, is often the source of his own self-destruction. He says, "I'm practical. I'm practical." Now, in mathematics, and in science in general, that's tragic. People who are practical are intrinsically tragic, because they limit themselves to what they think is practical, whereas progress is always based on getting beyond being practical by making discoveries of principle, or discovering principles which had existed before, but you hadn't understood them.

Progress is the increase of the creative powers, of the individual mind, and of society. Practical people, therefore, tend to be stupid people, not because they're inherently stupid, but they refuse to look to higher levels of challenges for success, for mankind: *success for mankind*. Which means it's another. It's not something you own, it's not something that's contained with inside you. It's something which if you adapt to it, and understand it, makes mankind more powerful in his own domain.

Speed: OK, so I think that's it for today. I want everybody to join me in thanking Lyn for an amazing Q&A. [applause] All right, Lyn, so we'll see you next week!

LaRouche: I hope! If I'm still living! [laughter]